CHANCES AND CHOICES

FURTHER TALES OF
A GENTLE SOUTHERN MAN

Jackie K. Cooper

By

JACKIE K COOPER

Southern Charm Press

Copyright © 2001 by Jackie K. Cooper
All rights reserved.
Southern Charm Press, 150 Caldwell Drive, Hampton, GA 30228
Visit our Web site at www.southerncharmpress.com

The publisher offers discounts on this book when purchased in quantities. For more information, contact: toll free: 1-888-281-9393, fax: 770-946-5220, e-mail: info@southerncharmpress.com

Printed in the United States of America
First Printing: November 2001

Library of Congress Control Number
    LCCN 2001087682

Cooper, Jackie K.
    Chances And Choices/ Jackie K. Cooper

    ISBN 0-9708537-3-4

Author's photograph by Terry Wood

Illustrator for book cover by Carol King Pope

Cover design by Ginuwine Graphics

FOR GENNA

WHO COMPLETES THE CIRCLE

OTHER BOOKS BY JACKIE K COOPER

JOURNEY OF A GENTLE SOUTHERN MAN:
REFLECTIONS FROM THE ROAD

ACKNOWLEDGEMENTS

There is no way to thank each and every person who has helped create this book. And I know going into this that I am leaving someone out. Still I must make an effort to convey my thanks to a variety of people who have given me the support I needed to get this book completed.

They are: Tom Kyle who gave me the first opportunity to write a book. Kathy Williams, the Publisher of this book, who saw the possibility of a new set of stories. Misty Ackley who typed and typed and typed. Ed Williams III who inspired me with his humor and his heart. Bobby Branch and Millard Grimes who mentored me. My father Tomas B Cooper who was the original "gentle southern man". JJ and Sean who are the world to me. And as always, Terry, who took a chance and chose me.

TABLE OF CONTENTS

A Wreck Rearranged Priorities
Not Everyone Is A True Fan
Dad's Goodness Came Naturally From Every Bone
In His Body
Surviving Labor and Delivery
Modern Families Also Have Modern Problems To
Face
Lightning Commands Respect
It's How You Play The Game
It's Enough To Drive You .. .. ..
It's Time To Be Thankful
Day Off Is A Day At The Mall
Holidays Aren't Always Merry
Anticipate But Don't Expect

Days Are For Dozing
Are You Flunking Out Of Relationships
Equality Begins At Home
Symbol Remains The Same
Let's All Move To Akaga
See You In Church
No Matter If You Win Or Lose, It's How You Treat
The Kids
Parents Set The Rules
My Mother Still Lives In My Heart
Summer Has Its Own Rhythm
Marriage Didn't Include Movies
Feline Offers Felicitous Care

Camp Was A Wash-Out
Stage Set For "Methodist Miracle"
Faithful Automobile Retired
But Can She Deliver Pups?
Money Can't Buy It All
Cats Can Be Jailbirds Too
Time Flies By When You're Having Fun
Get Out Of Abuse Filled Relationship
To Pray Or Not To Pray Is A Big Issue
Birthdays Aren't Memorable
You Can't Believe Everything
Wasp Mounted As A Trophy
Some Will Believe Anything
There's A Light To Guide Us

Sad Movies Make Me Cry
Turn Around and They're Grown
'Y'all Be Careful Out There'
Beauty Is Inward And Outward
'If This Was Played Upon A Stage Now, I Could
Condemn It As An Improbable Fiction'
Sore Foot Put Forward
Father Doesn't Think All Women Are Bad
Laughter: The Best Medicine
To Sleep; Perchance To Dream
"Turn Around And They're Gone, Part 2"
Was It Business Or Pleasure?
Many Welcome Couple's Baby
Winning The Battle Of The Bulge
Do You Remember When. . . .?
Couple Has A Second Chance
Check Writers Checked Out
College Has Become His Second Home
There's No Place Like Home. . .Unless You Are A
College Freshman

PROLOGUE

In life everything is one of two things – chances or choices. There are those things we choose to do and there are those things that seem to happen to us at random. For example, meeting the girl of your dreams is usually a chance occurrence. Choosing to marry her is a specified choice. Asking some one on a date is a choice while falling in love is a chance. You get the picture?

Now some would say there are no "chance" occurrences in life, but that everything is guided by a Supreme Being. Still being the Baptist/Methodist that I am, I believe in free will or to use my new phrase "chance." And therefore I believe that some things do just happen to us.

I believe that deciding to have children is a definite choice. The capability is by chance. The sex of the child is definitely by chance. At least so far. And as we go along the journey of our lives we come to crossroads. In some of these decisions we have a choice but with others we just have to put ourselves out there and let chance take our hand.

When we look back at where we have been we see that in some instances we were in the right place at the right time. And in some instances we were in the wrong place at the wrong time. Life takes twists and turns that we all try to control but sometimes can't. We are set off down a road that has many pitfalls and brambles to make our way through. Or just when we think we can't plod through the muck and mire another moment the sun comes out and dries the road and makes it passable once more.

If we could see the future we would make all the right choices, but we don't. That is why chance is so important.

Things that we do are like ripples in a stream. They span out and touch the shore of other people's lives. Whether it be by choice or chance these things do happen. We do cause other lives to alter directions and move in different ways. That is what makes life so great – the not knowing.

I have always seen each day as a chance to have something amazing happen. Something that can come like a bolt out of the blue, can spin you around and leave you breathless. When I think of these "chance' occurrences I usually think of them as being good things. Maybe that is just my old optimistic streak pushing through.

Still the telephone rings and you wonder just who the wonderful person might be with what wonderful news. Or the mail comes and you have a letter from someone that is going to make your life richer and better. A chance is as available as the next second of your life. It does happen that quickly.

As I journey down the road of life I find the excitement builds from day to day. And in the years "1988, thru 1991," my boys were still young and the chances and choices were running rampant. I hope that in these stories I have included from those years that you too can see what great mysteries there are in life and how much fun it can be to get involved.

Read on and see how chances and choices influenced the journey of a gentle southern man.

JKC

FORWARD

For this book I chose writings from my "journal" during the period 1988 thru 1991. These years were a time of "chances" as my children were getting older and my life was still in a settling down phase. Still mystical magic was in the air and I had adventures that invigorated my life and made each day a miracle. They were ordinary miracles but miracles of enjoyment just the same.

My "journal" filled up quickly during these times and the stories touch my heart when I re-read them over and over again. Now I pass them on to you for your observation and your enjoyment.

CHAPTER ONE

A Wreck Rearranged Priorities

Life does get complicated and complex at times. The every day existence of bills and bothers tends to wear one down. At least it does me. I go in cycles of panicking over money matters. Some days I am immune to debt worries while at other times I am obsessed by the wolf at the door.

Still when I am my most obsessive, and driving my family crazy about the money flow at our house, something comes along to make me rethink my priorities. Last week the reminder came in the form of a damaged car.

To set the record straight let me quickly say that my wife is one of the best drivers in the world. She is careful, cautious and alert. She drives the speed limit and obeys all the rules of the highway. Plus she always uses her seat belt.

Having gotten all that said I will proceed with my story. On the day in question I had come home from work sick with the flu. To help pass the time I decided to update my ledger. I keep a ledger with every entry as to what is spent on finances. I have it broken down by subject matter and cross reference with check numbers and dates. Doesn't everyone?

By the time my wife arrived from work, I was in a snit and a fit. Money was pouring out of our house in a flood of spending. Wasn't anyone else concerned? Was I the only sane person around? Didn't we have to stock up for the future lean years? Didn't Nostradamus predict an upcoming economic depression?

My wife tried to assuage my fears with calm reassurance but I wasn't buying it. I was determined that money matters were going to take a turn for the better soon.

Failing to get me in a better mood my wife left to get our sons from school. She had only been gone about fifteen minutes when the phone rang. It was her. "I'm alright," she said, "but I have been in a wreck."

Someone had pulled in front of her and caused a collision. Our car was damaged but she wasn't hurt. She had been going the speed limit. She had been wearing her seat belt. She had done everything right.

Aside from her not being hurt there were a million other things to be thankful about. She had been driving the Oldsmobile and not my compact Dodge Colt which she does sometimes drive. She had not yet picked up the boys so they were not in the car with her. Plus if my 15-year-old had been in the car he would have been driving and he surely doesn't need the trauma of a wreck at this young age.

Of course he is the philosophical member of the family. "Look at it this way, Dad," he said, "In a way it is good we have had this wreck. Now we are safe for a while since statistics show the average family has one wreck every five years." My mind must be able to adapt to teenage logic because somehow that did make sense to me.

So now we have the hassle of filing insurance claims, getting a rental car, and all the other headaches that go along with a car wreck even when it is not your fault. But I can handle it. My priorities are back in order.

They say when it rains it pours and money matters had turned into a hurricane for me. But the rainbow that came was the knowledge that personal health and safety of your family are all that really matter. The things that money can't buy are the things that make life worth living.

Not Everyone Is A True Fan

Insomnia is a funny disease. You may have partial insomnia, sporadic insomnia, or total insomnia. I am the victim of sporadic insomnia. I never know when it is going to hit. It can come at me without warning and leave me lying in my bed reviewing the past week, the past decade, or the sum total of my life.

My wife does not understand insomnia. She says sleeping is simple. You get in bed, you close your eyes, you go to sleep. That is easy for her to say. She has slept through tornadoes in Georgia, hurricanes in Florida, and earthquakes in California. When it is time to sleep, she sleeps.

The only sure cure for my sleeplessness is to sleep in front of a fan. That means an actual fan, situated at bed level, blowing directly on me. My wife does not think that remedy for insomnia is either healthy or sane. We compromised and put in a ceiling fan. It is not the same.

It all started in childhood. Back in those days we did not have air-conditioned houses. We had open windows and electric fans. My own personal fan, bought with love from caring parents, looked like a propeller from a fighter aircraft. You couldn't turn it on high speed and look into the face of its force. Your eyes couldn't take the pressure.

At night when I turned it on me its sound blotted out the outside world and its cooling currents transported me to another time and place. I loved it, I adored it, I became an addict. If possible I would have stayed in front of that fan and slept 24 hours a day.

During the winters the fan ran on low with its face turned toward the ceiling. It acted as a heat circulator. It wasn't as good as the summer effect but I still had the comfort of the noise and I could get a drift every now and then.

In college the fan drove my roommates crazy. It took three tries before I got one who could abide it. The man was a saint. The previous two had threatened to send me through the fan like a sausage grinder if I didn't come to my senses.

Finally I made it to law school. I was on my own. I had my own apartment. I could run my fan at will. And run it I did – summer and winter, seven days a week, twelve months a year. It purred by my side when I studied and it gurgled with delight when I relaxed.

During my third year in law school I moved into a furnished apartment. It had a four-poster bed, not with a canopy, but with four posts sticking up in the air. It was perfect. I tied a sheet to those four posts and turned the gust of the fan into it. The effect was like being on the ocean in the middle of a gale. I thought it was ingenious, others thought I was deranged.

On through life I sailed but eventually discovered I had to have more than just the companionship of a fan. I needed a partner for my life. I needed to be married. That's when the conflict began. Fans and family do not necessarily mix.

It never entered my mind I would have to give up my trusty fan when I got married. True my wife and I had not discussed my fixation with a fan, but I just didn't see how anyone could object to a practice that brought me so much pleasure and peace. I soon learned someone could and did.

I must have had some kind of premonition that the fan would not be accepted with open arms by my bride, for although I had the fan in the trunk of our car when we went on our honeymoon, I left it there. It didn't appear in our lives until we had returned home and were setting up housekeeping in our apartment.

By this time, I had traded in my airplane engine for a smaller model. It was still an open air fan with a wire screen through which you could stick your fingers and crank it if the engine was slow in getting started. This openness proved to be disastrous.

The fan had been relegated to my side of the bed. It sat there day and night like a noble guard. It was fiercely loyal to me and didn't like anyone else. I repeat – anyone else. My poor wife would go around to that side of the bed when she was making it up. Many times I would have left the fan running and it would literally charge her and chew at her nightgown.

One time I remember well. I had left for work but had to come back to the apartment to get something I had left. As I came in the door I heard all kinds of screaming and angry shouts. I stood in the door of our bedroom and observed a tug of war going on between my wife and the fan. The battle ended in a draw as the fan had to turn loose but it took some of the nightgown with it.

Saint that my wife is, she still allowed the fan to run at my side until one fateful night. I used to sleep with one foot out from under the covers so that I could feel the air currents stirred up by the fan. That night in my sleep I swung my foot around for some reason and it went into the back of the fan.

Now a fan's blades are set so you can not be injured if you strike them face on. You will only glance off them. But if you enter from behind they can cut and decapitate a finger or toe. My big toe went in from the back. It was a horrible awareness and jolt to my foot. My wife was immediately awake and questioning what had happened.

I tried to stay calm and tell her nothing had happened but I was also desperately feeling to see if my big toe was still attached. It was still there but it had been wounded. The telltale blood was on the wall. My fan had become public enemy number one and was banished from our room forever.

Later we moved into our home and got ceiling fans in just about every room. One we missed was the guest bedroom, which eventually became my youngest son Sean's room. To compensate for the lack of a ceiling fan I gave him a big box fan. He loves it. I do too.

Some nights when the insomnia gets too much for me I sneak into his room and curl up with my blanket in front of the fan. The air billows around me and the soft roar drowns out my cares. It works every time. I am asleep instantly and the sleep I get is fan-tastic.

Dad's Goodness Came Naturally
From Every Bone In His Body

"Father's Day" has come and gone and my gift has been sent to my father in South Carolina. This year he got a picture of me and my two sons. I thought that was kind of appropriate for "Father's Day." My wife Terry sent her father a picture of her with the two boys.

My father lives in Clinton, SC, and that is a small town. I imagine when people come to the house and see the gift they will naturally assume my wife and I are getting a divorce. Why else would she not be in the picture! I just hope my father doesn't have to spend hours explaining and declaring we are still together. They have already heard there is one divorce in the family (my brother's) and I know they are just waiting for the news about me.

Anyway "Father's Day" causes reflections back on my personal life with father. And in dwelling on those thoughts I bring up memories of a man who worked, and worked, and worked. He got up early in the morning and he worked until late at night.

The first job I remember him having was as a Pepsi-Cola salesman. It was great because I was a Pepsi drinker at that time. We were a family fiercely loyal to my father's products and to this day I feel a small pang of guilt when I reach for my Diet Coke.

At the time my father was working for Pepsi I thought he must be the strongest man in the world because he could swing those cases of Pepsi off the truck with ease. Maybe he was the strongest man in the world.

My father had been an athlete in high school. He played baseball, football and ran track. Poor man, neither of his sons inherited his athletic prowess. My father was such a good athlete that he was offered a scholarship to college. All he had to pay was $100, but his family did not have that hundred and my father went to work instead.

After Pepsi my father went to work as a bread salesman. He sold Merita bread. That bread sponsored "The Lone Ranger" radio and TV shows so I grew up with a sense of personal identification with that masked man. I was a member of the "Lone Ranger Fan Club" and I had a mask and silver bullet. Plus I never ate a sandwich which was not Merita bread through and through. People, I thought were our friends, used to try to sneak and buy another brand in the grocery store without us seeing them. But I saw, and I made mental notes as to their loyalty.

Being a bread salesman, my father went to all the stores in town, and naturally everyone in town knew him. And they all liked him. I mean they all, each and every one liked him. He was and is a man who inspires only kind thoughts in people.

At one time, I thought such goodness was only blandness but with maturity I have realized it for the excellent trait it is. It is hard to be nice and good without being a wimp and my father is no wimp. He is a gentleman, a gentle man.

I don't know how much my father and I are alike. Some people who know us both say there is a good bit of resemblance in looks and in traits. But I know I am not as good. I have to really work at being good. With my Daddy it comes naturally from the heart and from every bone in his body.

Surviving Labor And Delivery

When my oldest son turned 16 recently it was the cause of a great deal of reflection on my part. I found myself reliving the experiences surrounding his birth. Those were the days, 16 years that seem like 16 months or maybe even 16 weeks.

We were living in Rocky Mount, NC, during that time. I had just taken a job with Hardee's Food Systems as a real estate attorney. What that meant was I wrote contracts for the purchase of land on which to build Hardee's restaurants. It was a fairly good paying job and all the burgers I could eat. That was when my weight problems started.

We had only been in Rocky Mount a few months when we found out Terry was pregnant. I remember rushing into my boss's office and telling him I was going to have to have a raise. Poor man thought I had completely lost my mind – that is until I told him I was going to be a father. He immediately began to give me some father-to-be-advice, and he didn't give me a raise.

My father had told me that when the baby was born I was to call and tell him immediately. If for some reason he was not at home I was not to tell my stepmother. He wanted to be the first to know. Talk about putting you in a bind! My father was working then, he had not retired, so chances of him being at home when I called were pretty slim.

As it turned out the baby had to be induced. He was weeks overdue and all the walking around our apartment did nothing to encourage his birth. There had been some pains which I duly noted, but my notebook showed they were hours apart instead of minutes.

We were scheduled to go to the hospital on a Monday. I wheeled my wife in and they took her away. This was not one of those hospitals where the husband got to be in the delivery room. My space of operation was the waiting room. There I sat and smoked, and smoked, and smoked. I had given up cigarettes when we first found out we were going to have a baby, but now I started back with a vengeance.

Around noon, the janitor came into the waiting room. We started a conversation and he said I must be the man who had just had a son. Well I knew this wasn't true because I had just talked to a nurse and she said nothing had happened.

"You must have me confused with someone else," I said stiffly. "My wife has not had our baby yet."

"Oh yes she has, you have a little boy!" he demanded.

"No she hasn't!"

"Yes she has!"

And on and on it went until he said, "I am going back there and check."

I couldn't believe it but through those doors he went with his mops and bucket. I couldn't go through them but he could.

A few minutes later a nurse appeared with my son in her arms. She stuck his foot through a hole in a glass panel and I got to touch my son for the first time. It was the miracle to end all miracles.

While I stood there crying with joy the janitor pounded me on the back saying, "I told you that you had a son!" He had been the first to tell me and he had been right.

Within a few minutes I had placed a call to my home in Clinton, SC. My father answered the phone and I told him about his newest grandchild.

"Isn't that just like that sweet Terry," he said. "She had the baby on my lunch hour so I could hear about it first."

Sure Dad, sure.

Modern Families Also Have
Modern Problems To Face

The story you are about to read is basically true. I have changed the names and some of the circumstances to protect the innocent – and me. It sounds like something on a soap opera and if I had not heard of it first hand, I wouldn't have believed it.

The story came to me directly from my friend Trent. It was his monthly call to keep me informed on his family. Trent is one of those guys who has a modern family. There is he and his wife Dotty. Then there is his ex-wife Joan and her husband Charlie. Plus Trent and Joan's two kids live nearby. Daughter Katie is married and expecting Trent's first grandchild. Son, Scott, is involved in other adventures.

All of these people live in a radius of fifteen miles of each other, and they all communicate on a weekly, if not daily, basis. Joan's parents also live nearby. Her father is a Presbyterian minister and he tries to keep everything on a moral plane.

Trent is overjoyed about the approaching birth of his first grandchild. But he is not thrilled with Katie's behavior. She has fallen twice in the last week. Trent says it is sheer clumsiness. One time she was walking on the street after it rained and she slipped. Another time she was in the shower and slipped. Neither time was she or the baby hurt but Trent says one more slip up and he is taking the baby away from her. Obviously Katie doesn't know what valuable cargo she is carrying.

All of this was interesting, but I wanted to know the real purpose of his call. And that I found out was Scott. For some time now Scott has been seeing a young woman named Cindy. Cindy, according to Trent, is a good-time girl from the word go. Or to put it another way, Trent says she is a charter member of "Tramps-R-Us."

Scott and Cindy have been "living in sin" for about a year now. Everyone has tried to ignore it hoping it would go away, but it hasn't. They are still an item.

In June Scott graduated from college and asked his father for a trip to Hawaii for a graduation present. Trent balked at such an expenditure. But then ex-father-in-law, the minister, called him and said he would pay the $800 fare for Cindy if Trent would spring for Scott.

"But you would be condoning an out-of-marriage relationship," said Trent.

"Well, Scott just has his heart set on going to Hawaii and you know he wouldn't go without Cindy," said the grandparent side of the preacher.

"Why don't we just pay Scott $1600 to go alone and hope he meets somebody in Hawaii. There would be less chance of disease," said Trent. His ex-father-in-law was not amused.

So plans were made for the Hawaii caper. They were proceeding nicely when out of the blue Cindy's father called her. Now this man has not been heard from in years except for a child support check here and there. But suddenly he is the voice of sanity in an insane world.

He begged his daughter not to go to Hawaii unless she is married. She agreed if he would pay for the wedding. He agreed and suddenly Scott was engaged to the "Tramps-R-Us" queen.

Joan, Trent's ex, said she would have the rehearsal dinner if Trent would pay half. Trent agreed that sounded fair and made plans to send a check. But then it dawned on him that when he and Joan were married refreshments at a party they gave consisted of a can of Vienna sausages and some pop tarts.

I was very familiar with this brand of Joan's culinary talents because I was at that party and had eaten half the night's refreshments (five Vienna sausages) before I realized that one little plateful was all the food the party guests could expect. The other six people didn't get one sausage each.

This knowledge made Trent check with Joan to see what the menu would be. He found out her plans were for burgers in the backyard with butter beans and corn on the cob. That was quite a spread coming from Joan but Trent decided Scott deserved better.

Stepmother Dotty was even talked into planning the dinner and making reservations at a nice restaurant. Joan agreed it would be nice BUT Trent would have to pick up the entire bill. Trent agreed to feed the flock and still spring for half the honeymoon trip to Hawaii.

Plans were now going smoothly until it dawned on Dotty that something else was happening the night of the rehearsal dinner. It was scratching around the edge of her mind, but she couldn't quite put her finger on it. Then with a shriek her mind screamed, "Julio!" Yes folks, that Julio.

Julio Iglesias was going to be in their town on the night of the rehearsal dinner and Dotty had tickets for her and Trent. Nothing was going to mess up that night for her. She had been planning to see Julio live since she first heard him sing about "all the gerl he lubbed befur."

Now the battle lines were drawn. No Julio, no rehearsal dinner. How could it be resolved? Easily. Who says the rehearsal dinner has to precede the wedding on the immediate night. This wedding would have the rehearsal on Thursday, Julio on Friday, and wedding on Saturday. Solomon in his wisdom could not have solved it with more class.

The event will take place later this month. I think I will pass on taking it all in, and just let Trent fill me in later. He would prefer that I make the next one and let this one slide. He is sure there will be another wedding for Scott.

The reason I know is because of the last thing he said to me on the phone. It was "The sooner they get married, the sooner they can get divorced, and the sooner everyone can get on with their lives."

I think he may be fooled. Scott knows the worst about Cindy and it hasn't made any difference. Now he wants to have the best life possible. I am pulling for them to make it. For as Julio sings – all the previous loves aren't important. Only the current one is.

Lightning Commands Respect

From earliest childhood I have had a healthy respect for the power of lightning. To be honest I have had a total fear of it. When the storm clouds come and the lightning begins to boom you won't find me out and about. I seek the solace of home and protection of solid walls.

I really don't know why I have this fear. I know my mother also had it so maybe she passed in on to me. Her fear came because of a close call she had as a child. Even though I feared lightning I used to love to hear her tell about her brush with death by means of a "lightning ball."

In the house where she was reared there was a huge upstairs. It had to be since there were eight bedrooms and two baths up there. There were eight children in the family and four shared a bath. The rooms were arranged along a stretched out hall that ran from one end of the house to the other. The staircases went up and down to and from the second story at right angles so you had to turn off the hallway to get to or from the stairs.

Ventilation was aided by having a window at each end of the hallway. This kept a breeze moving constantly during the spring and summer. On the day of the "lightning ball" both windows were open.

Mother was up in her room and was unaware a storm had come up. The first awareness she had was when a loud clap of thunder sounded and shook the house. She wandered out into the hallway to see if anyone else was disturbed by the storm. No one was there.

She started down the hall when a burst of lightning came about and hit the power lines outside the window. A "huge" fireball ran down the line, and came straight in through the window. It was headed straight for mother, but her older sister Velma was also coming out of her room and pulled mother back into it with her and saved her life.

The fireball went straight down the hall and out of the window at the other end. Where it went then nobody knows. But mother and Aunt Velma always swore this was absolutely what happened.

Like I said this was one of my favorite stories my mother would tell. And she would always end it by saying that if Aunt Velma hadn't pulled her out of the way of that fireball she would have been "fried alive!"

Never wanting to be "fried alive," I made sure that when a storm came up I was always home and safe. If I couldn't be at home I was always told a car was the safest place to be. Those four rubber tires would protect you from harm.

On August 10, 1988, I found out how close one can come to being "fried alive," and also that a car is not man's best friend in a thunderstorm.

That night I had gone to Atlanta on business. I was headed home around 8 p.m. and decided to go by Conyers. I write for the newspaper there and wanted a copy for my files.

Conyers is a very nice place to visit but it is also the worst place for storms in Georgia that I know. The worst rainstorm I was ever in was in Conyers. The worst hailstorm I was ever in was in Conyers. Now I was heading there and little did I know but the worst lightning storm I would ever be involved with was taking place there.

When I got to Conyers that night the lightning was flashing all around me. But I kept saying to myself that

I was fine as long as I was in a car. I was protected. I was safe. Over and over I repeated this to myself as I drove to the front of the shopping center where there was a newsstand with a Conyers paper in it. It was right there in front of me, not ten feet from my car.

The storm seemed to subside, and for some reason I decided to rush and get my paper. I left the car running and the door open. I made it to the newspaper rack. I inserted my quarter. I got my paper. I turned around to head back to my car and – lightning struck my car!

It was a blinding flash, a sharp crack of thunder, and a knowing that it had happened. But it was all over in a second. I had missed being "fried alive" by being out of the car. For some reason I had been spared and I said a quick prayer of thanksgiving as I crawled back into my vehicle.

The car was still running, nothing smelled of being burned, everything apparently still worked, but I knew it had been hit. Still all I was concerned with was getting home. I wasn't going to sit there and examine the car detail by detail.

When I started out my mind was telling me something was wrong and then it dawned on me. I had no lights. That was what the lightning had struck. It had knocked my lights out.

Conyers is sixty or seventy miles from my home in Perry, and I had no lights. I also am no mechanic. My mind does not analyze what is wrong with a car and tell me how to fix it. It just doesn't work that way. So I tried the Jackie Cooper method of repair – I flipped the blink switch on and off hoping it would jiggle the light back on.

That did tell me something. I may not have had dim lights but I did have bright lights. So off I went to Perry with my lights set on bright and people cowering from the glare. I decided it would be best to take the back roads as I wouldn't meet too many people and permanently blind them.

Just as I reached the outskirts of Conyers the sky opened up. The rain began to come in sheets. I could hardly see the road. But if I thought I had trouble I knew the people meeting me head on were in worse shape. They had to contend with the blinding rain AND my bright lights.

I would see them coming down the road toward me and they would begin to wobble in the road. As they got beside me they would roll down their windows and yell obscenities in my ear. Or they would make their feelings known with gestures using their fingers or fists. It was not a pretty sight.

Finally the rain stopped as I reached McDonough. At this point I decided to move to the interstate for the rest of my journey home. I might still be blinding people by my brights but I would know the road better. It had to be a better journey from that point on. As I found out I was wrong again.

When I reached the interstate outside of McDonough, I found it to be pretty empty of cars. I eased onto the road and then it came alive. Cars and trucks came from everywhere. And there I was in the middle, bright lights illuminating the night.

That was bad enough but then the sky opened up again. The rain came down in torrents and the heat from the road surface created a steaming effect. When my bright lights hit it I felt like I was driving through cotton. It was a surreal experience and one I do not want to ever repeat.

The shower was a brief one and soon my only problem was the force of my lights in the rear view mirrors of my fellow drivers. At least I thought that was my only problem but drivers on the other side of the interstate were blinking their lights to tell me to cut mine back to dim.

I got behind one truck and couldn't pass him as there were cars on either side of me, going my same speed. I knew he didn't like the brights in his rear view mirror by the way he stuck his hand out the window. I decided he must have been a meat cutter by profession and had lost four of his five fingers in an accident as only one was visible.

Seeing that his wave to me was not getting the desired results he next proceeded to turn on a spotlight he had affixed to his cab. The spotlight was turned about until he found the perfect angle for shining it in my face. Now we were both blinded, he by my brights and me by his spotlight.

I managed to find a way clear to pass him and sped down the road to get away from that light. Once I finally got in front of him he turned on his brights and gave me a dose of what I had given him. Oh well, turn about is fair play I guess.

Eventually I made it home to Perry. It had taken three hours for what is usually a two-hour drive. I told my wife and children what had happened but I could see on their faces they didn't really believe me. Lightning strike the car? Ha!

The next day my wife took the car to our friendly auto repair shop. The globes on the lights had to be replaced. The mechanic said it looked like they had been struck by lightning. God had sent me corroboration.

So the next time you are driving down a road and see some poor fool coming towards you with his lights on bright, don't blind him with yours. Show some patience. He might have just had his car struck by lightning. You never know.

And the next time you hear Vicki Lawrence singing about "The night the lights went out in Georgia," listen a little more carefully. You might hear me singing these new lyrics, "That was the night my lights went out in Conyers. That was the night they cursed an innocent man!"

It's How You Play The Game

No matter how much modernists try to do away with the institution of marriage, it is alive and well and flourishing in the year 1988. People are rushing into it in record numbers and if it doesn't work out they are willing to try it again and again and again.

Not for me. I am happy, happy, happy in the marriage I have now so I could never settle for anything less. And I just don't think I could ever be this lucky again.

Plus I have known people who were involved in bad marriages. And from what they tell me when a marriage is bad it is terrible. Yet people who have escaped from bad situations often find themselves jumping back into the marriage trap once more.

I think time makes the mind forget how bad, bad was. Plus there is the stigma society places on anyone who is over 18 and single. At one time society allowed males to be unwed and envied but not anymore. Now if a male chooses not to marry there has to be something wrong with him. And we all can guess what that something is.

A single woman on the other hand does not usually have her sexual preference questioned; she has to live with the opinion of others that no man wanted her. It can never have been her choice not to wed. No! It is obvious that no man ever asked her.

I have a friend named Mary Ann. She is over 40 and single. In truth she would like to be married but she isn't. Years ago she was asked but said no. She thought true love would come along. It didn't. And there haven't been any askers in a long time.

Mary Ann is one of those women that society early on decided was "old maid" material. She has always been attractive but was never a raving beauty. But then a lot of married women aren't Miss Americas. The problem with Mary Ann was that she never learned to play the game.

The game never really had anything to do with looks or morals or intelligence. It was knowing how to make anyone and everyone feel that they were the special one. Girls are taught it from birth and the ones that don't learn become the Mary Anns of tomorrow.

There was a girl I knew in college who refused to play the game. She had her instructions at home but she just flat wasn't interested. Up until her senior year she was herself and to heck with what people, men especially, thought. But somehow in that senior year it hit her that she wanted an M.R.S. with her B.A.

She changed her hair style. She slimmed down her figure. She put on some makeup. But mainly she changed her attitude. She put the game into action and was engaged by the first semester. I haven't seen her since college so I don't know if it was worth it to her or not.

Still I suppose it was. Most women, and men, want the security of marriage. They want to be able to show the world that someone wanted them, that they were chosen. They don't want to end up like my friend Mary Ann.

Our minds tell us this "marriage premium" attitude is not right but it is the only game in town. Marriages come and marriages go but the eye is always on the next train away from being single. We live in an adult world of couples and it has been that way ever since Noah started moving them onto the ark.

It's Enough To Drive You ....

Cars are not my thing. I appreciate the fact that they run, but how and why they do is a big mystery to me. I am no mechanic. I wish I was but I am not. There are three cars in our family. They are all strangers to me.

A week or so ago I was on my way home from work. I had left right on time and had visions of a nice nap before supper. I am always planning for this nap but it always seems something happens to delay, postpone, eliminate it from my life. If I am going to take it, it has to be around 6 p.m. because if I go later than that I get my second wind and am awake until midnight or 1 a.m.

Anyway this day I was right on schedule for the 6 p.m. nap. That is until I got three blocks from my house and saw my son and his car on the side of the road. I could hear the nap saying bye-bye as I stopped my car and went to where my son was standing.

The car had sputtered and stopped he said which indicated to my feeble mind that it was out of gas.

"No way," my son insisted. "I had six more miles on the gauge before it could possibly be out of gas."

Do you remember being that young? That you measured your gas consumption not by the gas gauge but by the number of miles you had ridden.

Well obviously the number of miles lied because that car was flat out of gas. It wouldn't start for anything or anybody. So off we went to get some gas.

The container my son possessed with which to get the gas was battered to say the least. Three sides were caved in so that where it was supposed to hold a gallon of gas, a half gallon was a tight fit.

Back with the gas, we poured it in. The angle was a little awkward but it did appear to be tricking down inside the vehicle. But where it went I don't know. The engine still refused to come to life. It coughed and sputtered and died. It died so much that the battery soon went dead. Now we had to use jumper cables to try to bring the battery to life so that we could try to get the car to start. This was a bad day going worse fast.

That's when the angel of mercy appeared. She drove by, saw us, and stopped. She hopped out of her car, ran over to where we were. Gave a "Hi, Cooper" to my son and preceded to look under the hood.

I was a little wary of teenage girls who look under hoods. Especially one as pretty as this young lady. I explained our problem to her and said, facetiously, "I hope you are a mechanic at heart."

"I am," she quickly replied, and then proceeded to check various and sundry parts of the vehicle. She called them all by name and impressed me and my son.

Call me a chauvinist but I never thought a petite girl could know so much about how a car works. She suggested that we try this and she suggested that we try that. None of it got the car started but it all made sense.

Just when I was ready to call for the tow truck she volunteered to get her father who, she said, really knew a lot about cars. She and my son took off while I stood guard over the car. Don't you hate standing on the side of the road with a car that won't go! People pass by and look at you like you are either crazy or pitiful. I felt both. I was pitiful crazy to be missing my 6 p.m. nap for the convenience of a car. I should have just called a tow truck and let it go at that.

But soon the young lady, her father and my son were back. The father was as nice as the daughter and knew worlds about cars. At least it seemed so to me.

Four heads went under the hood. Three knew what was going on and one didn't.

"Do you know anything about cars?" asked the father.

"Not a thing," I replied. I never try to bluff it about cars. I figure what the heck. If I am a dummy, then I'm a dummy. I have my own fields of expertise – movies, television and plays. To each his own I say.

Anyway this was not one of those guys who looks down their noses when you plead ignorance. He just smiled and went about the business of getting the car started. And while he did it he gave further instructions to his daughter. He would test this and that and while he did he would remind his daughter of what he had told her about each and every part.

Now this was a good relationship. The father was instructing the daughter but he wasn't lecturing her. He let her know that he wanted her to learn but he also showed her he respected her opinion. I was impressed with his knowledge and with his relationship with his daughter.

Finally the only option came down to going for more gas and giving it another try. I was stationed with the car again while the rest went off for gasoline.

In just a few moments they were back. The father had discovered he had a gasoline can at the house and it was full of gas. It was quickly placed in the gas tank and lo and behold the car started.

I was so pleased I didn't know what to do. I offered my thanks in profusion and I begged to pay for the gasoline the father had provided. He graciously accepted my thanks but refused my money.

This man and his daughter lived out the story of the Good Samaritan. No, my son and I were not beset by robbers but we were in need of aid and they provided it. They did it without hesitation or hope of profit.

In this day and age when you read so much about the horrors of the world it is nice to know kindness still exists. Tennessee Williams had Blanche Dubois speak of "the kindness of strangers" in his play, "A Streetcar Named Desire." I had always liked that phrase and with this incident I truly learned what it was like to be dependent on the kindness of strangers.

Well we are no longer strangers. As we were saying good-bye the father looked at me and said, "It just dawned on me. You are the one who writes!"

Yes that is me and I am glad writing has given me the opportunity to thank this man and his daughter. And to let you know that good people still exist in this world. If that bit of knowledge doesn't make your day, nothing will.

It's Time To Be Thankful

We are fast approaching the holiday season and for those of you know me, you know the holidays put me in a blue funk that lasts from Thanksgiving through New Year's Day. So before I am crushed by the weight of holiday cheer, I'd like to give you my list of things for which I am thankful.

First off I am thankful for God, country and health. I always have to say those first and get them out of the way. Not that they aren't important, they are. Its just if I don't automatically say them first I have a bad case of the guilts.

Okay, I am also thankful for my friends; past, present and future. Some have disappointed me, some have inspired me, some have abandoned me and some have stood beside me. All of them have affected me in some way or another.

I am thankful for my parents, all three of them. My mother and father did some things wrong and some things right. My stepmother did some things wrong and some things right. But in total what they did was alright because I turned out alright.

I am thankful for my in-laws and what they did wrong and right in raising their daughter. They did OK too because she is great.

I am thankful I grew up in the South and that I live in the South today. No matter how you look at it the South is the greatest place in the world to raise kids. You still get a sense of family and community that just doesn't exist anywhere else.

I am thankful California exists and that I had two years of living out there. It still exists in my mind as the most magical place on earth and I will always be in awe of it. The earthquakes and the smog convinced me I wasn't cut out to be a California resident but it is the best place to visit.

I am thankful my wife was willing to pack up and move with our two small children out to California. She gave me two years of that state and enough memories to last a lifetime. She also had the sense to know when it was time to come home, and I guess I am thankful for that too.

I am thankful for divorce. That ought to send you scurrying for the phone. No I am not getting a divorce and I have never been divorced. But some of the people I love the most have been, and for most of them it was the right thing. Now they have had the opportunity to find the right person and to have the happiness they deserve. I don't want anyone I love to be miserable and divorce has been a way some misery has been ended and some great happiness has been found.

I am thankful for my church. It is the institution that makes me the angriest and also gives me the most comfort. Flawed though I think it is, I am thankful every day that it exists.

I am thankful for movies, television shows, plays and concerts that bring me happiness in excess. And I am grateful for sports events that bring my children and friends such happiness. And I am thankful that my friends and family accept that sports do not bring me the happiness movies do.

I am thankful I fell in love for the first time at 16 and learned what love was all about. This love prepared me to fall in love again 10 years later and have it be the greatest one of all.

I am thankful for my children because I can see eternity through their eyes.

And I am thankful I am me. I don't think anyone else could cope with being me or would enjoy it half as much.

Happy, happy Thanksgiving!

Day Off Is A Day At The Mall

So how did you spend the day after Thanksgiving? Did you curl up in your favorite chair and watch TV and nap? Did you fill yourself with leftover Thanksgiving Day food and wallow in your new found weight? Did you bask in the glow of family and friends and enjoy that day off from work that gave you a loooong weekend? Not me! I spent my day at the mall.

When they give out the good husband award the address is 2017 Laurel Drive. That's where I – superhusband – live. Now I know I will have to share it with some other poor slobs that I saw wandering glassy-eyed around the mall, but just make sure my name is engraved with the rest for all to see.

The quest my wife and I engaged in at the mall was for the "perfect dress." Now she didn't know what it looked like, though she had a general idea, but she knew when she saw it the bells would chime and the stars would shine.

So off we went to the mall. We left bright and early without a bite to eat or even a cup of coffee. We were dedicated shoppers. But so it seems were ten million other people. They bore down on that space of ground called the mall and covered it like the dew in Dixie.

Alone and separate these may have been nice people. But in a vehicle headed for the mall they were crazed drivers hunting for a parking space and God help anyone or anything that got in their way.

Finally we managed to find an empty space, two blocks over from the mall. Now we only had to negotiate the roads and parking lot to get to the stores. Cars racing for parking spaces do not look out for pedestrians.

Inside it was twilight zone time. The whole world had come to my mall to shop. It was shoulder to shoulder and glare to glare. I was swept along from store to store without having to use much of my own power.

Inside the stores you would see the men scattered here and there as their wives dashed hither and yon. Most of the men there were of the newlywed variety. They were fresh-faced and starry-eyed. The glow was still surrounding them as they oohed and aahed over everything the woman in their life brought forward.

Then there were the veterans. These were the men who came armed with newspapers, magazines, candy bars and comfortable shoes. They moved with a sluggish pace and kept a roving eye for any spare chair that might appear. Some even folded up and sat on the floor at the feet of the dressing room doors.

Now why is that? Why can't a store get smart and provide chairs for the poor spouses that are along on these buying trips. In 14 stores we entered only two had any kind of seating arrangement. That is rank discrimination. It also antagonizes the husband and makes him negative about any clothes on sale there.

We finally found our quarry in a store with a chair. After standing in line for ages to get inside a dressing room, my wife appeared in "the dress." Bells did ring and stars did shine. She was a happy woman.

We placed "the perfect dress" in the trunk of the car and went in search of food. After we had eaten I almost felt human again. I also begin to think about the plusses of the day. I had walked off some weight. I had made my wife happy. And most of all I had enough guilt ammunition to use on her for the next three months. All in all it wasn't a totally wasted day.

Holidays Aren't Always Merry

Even though many of the songs of the holidays say this is the season to be jolly, for many of us this is the worst time of the year – emotionally speaking. Why the most joyous season of the year should work in reverse is a mystery. But it does have that effect on some people.

Now all my life I have been one of those people whose life is full of highs and lows. When I was younger the highs were higher and the lows were lower. But then I was more self-indulgent in my youth. If something hit me wrong I would wallow in self pity and thoroughly enjoy my miserable feeling.

On the other hand I would be on top of the world if I found a dime in the dirt or my *TV Guide* came on time. It didn't matter how big the treat was as long as it was something I considered to be a treat.

Sometimes I think the mood swings in my high school and college days were a little calculated. I could use them to get my way or to fend people off if they got too close. Whatever the reason I continued to be a person of highs and lows until after I married.

Today I still have moments of euphoria I can not explain and I also have periods of depression that can't be nailed down to any specific occurrence either. Luckily they aren't severe. I stay on a pretty even keel.

Others are not as lucky. One lady I know counts the days of Christmas, not in anticipation but in dread. As the numbers draw down she feels she has fewer days to make her way through and she lives for Jan. 2 to arrive. In her case the holidays remind her of the death of a parent and every Christmas event is just a symbol of her loss.

Another friend of mine sees the holidays as a season to get through because it increases his isolation. He has never been a person who made friends easily and at Christmas time his inability to be sociable is intensified. He is unmarried and lives away from the town where his parents reside. They are not close to him anyway so he doesn't make the obligatory trip home. He used to do that and it was a disaster.

So he stays alone and endures the season. It is not easy. The world cries out about its love in every song and slogan but he feels it is all a sham. Holed up in his own little corner of the world he doesn't share in any rosy glow.

I could go on and on with examples of people who do suffer the pangs of the damned with depression. Perhaps their condition is not bad enough to be treated, or they don't want to admit it is. Or they think it is all mental and they can exorcise it with positive thoughts.

Whatever it is or whatever causes it, it is real. When it hits me I try to stay busy. If it gets worse, I search for my favorite things to do. And the third stage is to get with my wife or best friend and talk it out. Talking seems to be one of the best ways to get it out of your system.

If you know someone who has trouble at Christmas getting the holiday spirit, don't make fun of them. They may be making the best effort they can. Use a little of your Christmas caring to help them make it through to the bright calmness of January. The Beatles song says, "I get by with a little help from my friends. I get high with a little help from my friends," to that you could add, "I get out of my lows with a little help from my friends."

Anticipate, But Don't Expect

During the holiday season the air is filled with anticipation. There are so many things to look forward to – the decoration of the homes, the music by the church choirs, the visits from your family, the many special events that take place. And for me the anticipation of these events is sometimes better than the events themselves.

I learned long ago that anticipation is one of the best feelings in the world. Because with anticipation anything can happen. You can anticipate winning a million dollars in the sweepstakes or you can anticipate oil being discovered in your backyard. That is the wonderful thing about anticipation, the possibilities are only limited by the imagination in your brain.

The first time I think I ever became aware of the joy of anticipation was sitting in a movie theater. The previews of coming attractions were on and all of the movies being advertised looked great. I could just imagine the joy I was going to have seeing those films. I went over and over it in my mind and lived the future experience in advance.

Later in life I began to plan my career. I sent out applications and letters to various places for a variety of jobs. With each letter I sent I lived in my mind what would happen if this certain place or person hired me. I dreamed of the work and I dreamed of the salaries. The anticipation was the best part of the search.

Now there is a distinct difference between anticipation and expectation. Anticipation as I said is a form of joy. Expectation generally leads to disappointment. When I was watching all of those previews if I had expected the movies to be great then I probably would have been in for a let down when I saw them. Expectations rarely are exceeded.

A few years ago a friend told me how she was looking forward to her son graduating from college, meeting a nice girl, falling in love, getting married, settling down, and giving her grandchildren. This was her form of anticipation and she was having a wonderful time living her dreams day by day.

Now we move forward to the present. I saw her last week and she told me Robert was getting married. She didn't seem happy. I knew he had been dating a girl from California and thought my friend liked her. The girl had been to her home for several visits and appeared to be an answer to any mother's dreams.

"Don't you like the girl he is going to marry?" I asked.

"I did," was the response. "I liked everything about her. In my dreams she and everything about her were perfect."

"So what went wrong," I asked back.

"I expected them to stay here when they got married. I never expected the hussy to marry him and make him move away from me," said the mother of the future groom.

My friend should have learned what I learned long ago. Expectations are deadly. You always want more and expect more than you are ever going to get. People and events will let you down if you expect too much. Better to anticipate everything but expect nothing. That's my motto and when I have practiced it, it has worked like a charm.

Chapter 2

Days Are For Dozing

All of my life I have had my days and nights mixed up. Or maybe it is just that I am a night person rather than a day one. Anyway it has always been that I sleep my best, my deepest sleep during the daylight and fight going to sleep at night.

How I envy my wife, her ability to fall asleep as soon as her head hits the pillow. I lie there and relive my day, the past week, the past month or even the past year. I plan for the future and think up a million things I am going to do. If something is bothering me I analyze it over and over.

When I finish with my soul searching it is generally really late. Then I begin to panic. I have got to go to sleep, I have got to go to sleep, my mind keeps telling me. And the more it says it, the wider awake I am.

But not so during the day. If I am off from work and it is 2 or 3 in the afternoon I can sail off to sleep and the thunder of cannons can not wake me up. It is indeed the sleep of the dead.

Several months ago Sean, my youngest son, and I were the only ones home in our house on a Saturday afternoon. He said he was going out to a friend's house and play ball. I told him to take his house key as we always keep our house locked tight as a drum. He said he was afraid he would lose it, so he didn't take it.

As soon as he was out the door I fell asleep. I didn't plan it that way, I was reading and I dropped off. The next thing I knew Sean was bending over me waking me up. It was three hours later from what I last remembered.

Sean had come home and rung the doorbell. That didn't work. He went to a neighbor's and called on the phone. I didn't hear it. After an hour or so he began to panic. Maybe, he thought, I was lying upstairs dead. Deciding my life was worth more than a window, he broke a pane and let himself in only to find me asleep.

For months this deep sleep event of mine was the subject of jokes around our house. But Sean now takes his key whenever he leaves. And nobody trusts me to let them in when I am in the house alone.

That should be enough writing about my sleep habits but it isn't. Over Christmas another event occurred. My brother was coming to our house from Florida. He was supposed to arrive at 5 in the afternoon.

Dumb me, I carried my book upstairs ad laid down on the bed to read around 3 p.m. Terry, my wife, called around 5:15 p.m. and woke me up. She asked if my brother had arrived yet. I responded that he hadn't. Fifteen minutes later I heard the doorbell ring. It was my brother.

He had arrived 45 minutes earlier. He had rung the doorbell, pounded on the door, hollered and screamed. I hadn't heard a thing. Finally he had gone on a walk around the neighborhood to pass the time until someone arrived and let him into the house.

If he had arrived at our house at 5 a.m. it probably wouldn't have been a problem at all. I am such a light sleeper at night that I hear everything. But those daytime naps are when I really go out like a light.

So if you're awake late at night and need someone to talk to, give me a call. Chances are I'm awake. But don't try to rouse me during my daytime sleepathons. The phone may ring; there may be pounding on the door; but I don't hear it. I am away in never-never land in the most beautiful sleep of all.

Are You Flunking Out
Of Relationships?

Don't you wish there was a school somewhere that offered a valid course in relationships. A place where you could take this course and all of your problems with spouse, kids, parents and friends would be resolved. Because if we could settle relationships there wouldn't be any problems left in the world. Well, maybe disease, famine and disasters would remain, but a big chunk of woes would be removed.

Just about everyone I know – no, make that a positive statement – everyone I know has a problem with one kind of relationship or another. And at the top of the list are relationships with parents. Young kids, teenage kids, young adult kids, and even grown kids have problems with their parents.

Take the case of my friend Skip. He is newly married to a wonderful girl. The only problem is she has a mother. And the mother lives close to where they do. So she is available to drop by, or drop in, or move in when the spirit moves her.

Last Christmas Skip's wife informed him that her sister and brother-in-law were coming to town to see them. They were brining their two kids. It would be a crowded Christmas at Skip's house. But good old Skip, he never said a word.

He didn't say a word when he learned he and wife were giving up their bedroom to the visiting couple. After all there was still the comfortable guest room. But it also was soon taken. It seems Skip's mother-in-law didn't want to miss out on all the fun of the family reunion. So she didn't want to spend Christmas at her apartment. She decided to move in for the holidays too.

Somehow Skip survived. He survived the company. He survived the bunk beds he and his wife finally occupied. But Skip has said, "never again!" His wife has agreed. But the mother-in-law is now playing the role of martyred woman. The relationship is messed up.

Another case in point is my friend Arnold. He is married and the father of grown children. He and his wife are happy and compatible. The only problem is Arnold's father. A more cantankerous old soul you would never want to meet. He never has a good word to say about anything.

Still, Arnold is a devoted son who puts up with this garbage day in and day out. Some loyalties are there just because the relationship is there.

Anyway, the other day Arnold, who is approaching 60 was talking with his son Kenneth. Kenneth was asking his father how in the world he put up with the old man. Arnold just shook his head and didn't have an answer.

Then he said, "Can't you just see Dad at 102 in perfect health, coming to my funeral."

Kenneth quickly responded, "Dream on, Dad. What makes you think he would even come to your funeral?"

I hear stories like this day after day. It makes me glad I have the relationship with my parents that I have. But even that good relationship can have its bad days. The lack of a phone call, or the wrong words said on the phone can get things off and running.

Somebody ought to start that school for relationships. We would all have to enroll. Even the ones with the most glib tongues and smoothest speeches stumble on the road of relationships and find themselves knee-deep in potholes from time to time.

Equality Begins At Home

I was raised to be a bigoted chauvinist male. Now this was not an intentional thing on the part of my parents, it had more to do with the time and place where I was reared. I was a child of the '40s and '50s, and that was a time when the most you could ever hope to be was white and male.

Up until the time I went to law school at the University of South Carolina, I lived primarily in a segregated world. The schools I attended were all white and all of my social acquaintances were too. I don't think I was a conscious bigot, I just lived that way.

As far as chauvinism went, well that was the name of the game. Girls were pretty and sweet and mostly dumb. Oh there were some smart girls in my classes but they weren't overtly smart. They just lucked into those good grades.

Even the beloved cheerleader that I dated for years and years and years played the game of "second best" with a passion. I was always smarter, more popular, etc., or at least she felt it her total duty to make me feel that way. It was as close to being king of your own little country as you could get.

My view of the world as being composed of people of more than one color came about when I entered the Air Force. When I was assigned to OCS I had a black roommate. It was a disaster. I was so conscious of him being black and me being Southern that I couldn't carry on a normal conversation. I thought I was being nice, but in truth I was being totally condescending and he knew it.

Later when I was in one of my first jobs I worked with a racially mixed group of people. And when I was new in that office one of the people who helped me the most was Dave. He was older, more experienced in the work we did, and just totally and naturally nice. He saved me from making some big mistakes on more than one occasion.

One day a friend of mine came by the office. As we were leaving he asked me who the "nigger" was at the next desk. It sent me totally into shock. Not that I had never heard the word before, but I was shocked that someone would use it talking about Dave. I really think that is the closest I have ever come to hitting someone. I didn't hit him – though he was smaller than me. But I did tell him that I didn't work with any "nigger." And with that line I ended the friendship.

Years passed and I think I became more enlightened in several ways, but it took a strong headed but totally wonderful wife to make me see what women have gone through. She pointed out remarks that men and women made which placed women in a certain subservient category. My eyes were opened.

The other day a person called my office to talk to me. He had a question to ask and didn't think he had gotten the right answer from the "little girl" who worked for me. That "little girl" is a grown woman of 30 who is one of the most efficient people I have ever known. It was Dave time all over again. I saw red.

And before he continued I said very plainly and distinctly, "I don't have any little girls working for me." That's all, no ranting or raving. It probably went right over his head, but it made me feel better.

Some men have a need to have "little girls" in their lives. But I still feel like a king, sharing my kingdom with an equal partner.

Symbol Remains The Same

Way back at the dawn of creation when I was involved in the dating game, I gave my girlfriend a friendship ring. It was Valentine's Day and I wanted her to have some expression of my true love, so the gift was bought. In truth it was not a very expensive ring, just a little silver circle of hearts.

The problem was that the ring was cheap and it began to tarnish her finger. As a matter of fact it gave it a green glow. But until love died that ring was sacred. And I knew our relationship was really over when that ring came off her hand.

So why am I telling you this. It all happened a long time ago and has no bearing on my life today. But something happened recently to bring back the memory of "the ring." Something that made me remember how important that ring had been.

It happened at a movie. I was sitting there munching my popcorn and was wondering how they ever talked Tom Hanks into making a movie so bad, when I heard a conversation going on behind me. Conversation and much scuffling about under my seat.

Luckily at that time the movie ended and the lights came on and I could see that it was a young lady about 12 or 13 who was doing the hunting. Her older sister was helping her. She didn't seem to have as much enthusiasm for the task and was constantly saying, "Let's go!"

Being a helpful soul I asked what the problem was. "She lost her ring," said the older sister.

I joined in the search but I didn't seem to add much to the success rate. We put aside every box of popcorn and every candy wrapper in the area but nothing helped. The ring was not to be found.

"Come on, Nancy. Let's go." Said the sister again, tugging at her arm.

"Just let me look a little bit more, please. I can't let Danny know I lost his ring. I just can't," Nancy said looking like she was on the verge of tears. "He'll think I didn't take care of it or didn't like it."

By this time I had gotten a flashlight from the usher and was using it. But still no ring appeared. It looked like the ring, and maybe Danny, would be lost forever.

The older sister renewed her demands to leave and slowly Nancy went up the aisle and out of the theater. It was a painful sight to see her walking out so dejected and I made a silent prayer in my heart that the ring would turn up.

As I went back to my seat I stepped on something. I looked down and it was a tiny silver ring with hearts in it, laying on the floor. It was in a place where I had looked several times, but this time it was there.

I scooped it up and raced out of the theater and got to Nancy just as she was getting into her car. Her smile lit up the night like neon. And to her sister's credit, she was smiling too.

Maybe the three of us just weren't careful enough in our looking. Or maybe an angel heard the prayer of a young girl and an older man who remembered the value of rings and things. Whatever the reason a ring appeared on the floor in a place where it had not been previously, and found its way back to the finger of a young girl lost in her first love.

I believe in rings and things. I believe in first love. And I believe in miracles.

Let's All Move To Akaga

Recently I was reading one of those "question and answer" columns that appear in the newspaper. The question concerned President George Bush wanting to be the leader of a country called "Akaga." The person asking the question wanted to know where this country is located.

Now I am not an expert on geography. If I was ever to appear on "Jeopardy" that would not be one of the categories I would jump at. But I do know where "Akaga" is. Do you?

When I was a little boy I lived in the secure world of Clinton, SC. I lived there with my father, my mother, and my brother. We lived in a house with two bedrooms and one bathroom. It also had a living room, a kitchen, a screened-in side porch and a wonderful hall where the oil furnace was located.

In my memories it is generally always summer there. But I do remember some rare snows and some rainy days. When I think of the rainy days I remember the big gullies in front of our house and how the water would come swooshing down through them. My brother and I would take little boats and start them floating at one end of the block and race them through the gullies to the other end.

During the summer nights we would play baseball in the streets, stopping when cars would ride by. Sometimes it was just the neighborhood kids but on other times our fathers would join us. Even though they had been working hard all day they would still find the energy to play. And in these neighborhood games it was just play-for-plays sake. No hard-nosed competition, no stress, just fun. And under these circumstances even I was an OK player.

Later in the evening the kids would gather under the streetlight to tell ghost stories. And there we would be until we had to run home to use the bathroom or until our mothers called us in for the night. Sometimes we would pretend we had to go to the bathroom so we wouldn't have to hear the scariest part that the older kids would tell.

On Sundays we went to church. Everybody in the neighborhood did. Most of us were Baptist but there were a few Methodists or Presbyterians. I always liked going to church because when I was real little it was a great place to sleep. They had big fans on the ceiling and I could stretch out on the pew and go to sleep while the preacher talked about Jesus and Heaven.

Church was a constant in my life. The same people were there week after week and the same preacher was there year after year. I only knew one preacher the whole time I was growing up. He was at our church for 28 years. That's the way the Baptists do things. Now I am a Methodist and we don't keep a preacher more than four years as a general rule.

That's what it was like growing up in the '40s and '50s. It was a place of security and a place of family. It was a place of religion and a place of caring. At least in the neighborhood where I lived.

The writer wanted to know about the country of Akaga, the place where George Bush wants to be president. The answer was that Akaga means "A kinder and gentler America."

The reason I know about Akaga is that I grew up

there.   Does it exist now? Well sometimes I have my doubts. But for the sake of my children, and all children everywhere, I hope it will exist again.

See You In Church!

Last weekend my brother-in-law and his wife were visiting with us. Whenever they come up to see us from Florida it seems we get into a talk marathon. We analyze, dissect, ponder, and proclaim about every subject under the sun. We talk and talk and talk

Last weekend was no exception. We talked from the time they arrived on Friday until they left on Sunday. And on Saturday night we talked into the wee small hours of the morning. Plus we lost an hour to Daylight Savings Time. So when we went to bed at 3 a.m., it was actually 4 a.m.

The whole reason for this background is to explain why we didn't go to church on Sunday morning. Now that may not seem to be such a big thing to some people, but it is to me. I like going to church. It makes my week start off right. It is a tradition in my family as well as a habit.

I once told someone I went to church out of habit and they lashed out about my lack of commitment and depth of Christianity. I shrugged it off as their problem. My "habit" has nothing to do with my faith. It exists whether I go to church or not. But getting up and going to church on Sunday morning is a habit I have had since childhood, and one I want to instill in my children.

Let's face it, getting up and going to church is not always the most wonderful option we have on Sunday morning. There are many, many times when I would have preferred to stay in bed and sleep. Haven't you felt that way?

When I was a child there were many times when I would beg not to have to go to church. I could pretend sickness with the best of them. The problem was my mother could always see right through me.

When I went to college I had it in the back of my head I wouldn't be going to church anymore. That would be reserved for trips back home. And for the first few weeks, or maybe a month, I didn't go. Then the old guilt kicked in. Somehow I couldn't sleep 'til lunch time and then lurch to the dining hall and eat my meal without guilt. The day just didn't seem right.

Slowly but surely I began to get up for Sunday School and church. It became the natural thing to do once again and I know it was because of the "habit" I had formed when I lived at home.

There were other times when I was single that I would begin to slip from the routine. In each case my upbringing and my need to be part of the Sunday worship would always resurface and get me back. It wasn't that my faith faltered but only that my routine got altered.

I feel fortunate that my wife shares my desire to go to church each Sunday. I know many people whose spouse does not go. In those instances where the other member of the marriage continues on, they have my total respect. They are really dedicated.

Old habits die hard and I guess that is what my parents relied upon. They made sure I expected to go to church each and every Sunday. It hasn't worn off in all these years and I don't think it ever will.

No Matter If You Win Or Lose, It's How You Treat The Kids

If you were to make a list of those persons who have most influence over your children's lives you would include parents, peers, teachers and preachers. And if your child is involved in sports you should put coaches at the top. For coaches affect children in direct and indirect ways that last a lifetime.

High school, college and professional coaches are under a lot of pressure. If they don't win they get fired. The theory of enjoying the games has just about gone out the window.

When I was in high school my best friend Hollis was a star basketball player. He wasn't a 6-foot giant but he was quick, he was smart, and he could shoot.

When it came time to go to college he asked me to ride with him to a school where he was going to try out for a basketball scholarship. All of his dreams were to play college basketball. He had it all planned in his mind.

The first thing the coach said to him at the meeting was, "You're too short for college basketball."

Hollis didn't play college basketball. His try-out that day was pathetic. He had been psyched out by a coach with no sense of the right thing to say. Maybe he wasn't college material, but maybe yet he was. In either event the negative introduction given by the coach wiped him out. And I think he still feels the scars to this day.

Now I didn't play high school basketball. When I was in eighth grade I decided I would try out for the "B" team. I figured you didn't have to be really great to play there. And I was a fair player if not the greatest.

Well I went to all the practices, and I made the team. But I didn't get to play. Well, not play to any substance. I got to go in during the last five seconds or something stupid like that. But most of the time I was on the bench. When I would ask the coach he would say maybe next game. Then he would tell me to give him an extra five laps around the gym and I would get more game time – but I didn't.

After about four or five games like this I began to wise up. It became obvious I wasn't going to get any extra time of play. And this nutso was just enjoying seeing me race around the gym in hopes of impressing him.

So I quit the team. I can imagine the horror in your eyes right now. How could anyone be a quitter. It is not the American way. Well neither is humiliation and embarrassment. I was 14 years old and I was being made to feel like less than zero. I at first put all the blame on myself then I wised up. It was his problem. He had picked out the team he wanted and I was just in the way.

Treatment like this of children is a form of child abuse. It isn't the physical type you can see but it is the emotional kind that hides inside. When self worth is destroyed it may never be regained.

Some coaches are volunteer, some don't earn a lot, some do all right. But in all cases we give them our most prized accomplishments – our children. How they treat them is their most important goal. Bigger than winning games. Much bigger.

Parents Set The Rules

Sometimes it amazes me that I am now the parent and have children for whom I am responsible. It was only yesterday that I was in high school and couldn't understand why my parents were so concerned about what I did. I just knew that I knew best. I also knew that I was smarter than they were. So what was the problem? I was young, smart and invincible. Now that I look back I see that I was young – period.

So what is different now? Kids are still kids and parents are still parents. There are good kids and there are bad kids just like always. But there is a difference. We are the parents who grew up in the '60s and early '70s. And those were the good old years of live and let live – love and let love.

Somehow we thought love and good thoughts were going to carry us through. We wanted more freedom so we in turn gave it to our children when they came along. But we forgot to instill in them that freedom only survives when it is handled responsibly.

Today our children are awash in the freedoms we give them. We pride ourselves on how liberal we have become. We tell each other how we never interfere in our children's lives. We trust them, we say. And because we trust them we let them do basically what they want to do.

But it's not working. It isn't working because kids need guidance. They need guidance and we as parents need to be responsible. And being responsible means making rules. Then when rules are made they need to be enforced. Now don't get me wrong I am not talking about some kind of police state. Kids do have certain rights. But those rights must have boundaries.

It is unfair to expect a 14, 15, or 16 year-old child to make adult decisions. It's easier for the parent if the child has the duty to decide, but it is basically unfair to the child. Take the issue of drinking. I have had parent after parent say to me: "Well I am just going to leave it up to them. I am sure they won't abuse it. One beer isn't too much for a teen to drink."

Still who is going to tell that teen to stop after one drink? Their friends? Don't bank on it. So the one beer leads to two and then a few more and on and on. Maybe they will be able to handle it and maybe they won't. Or maybe they will become an alcoholic.

It does happen. I have a friend who thought it was fun for his son to drink some beer after him even when he was a little boy. And when he was in high school it was a great father/son event to share a beer together on a hot summer afternoon. But those drinking habits compounded and now the father can control his drinking habits, but his son cannot.

Look folks, I don't know all the answers. I have children and I make mistakes day after day. I am struggling through this parent thing just as you are. But we have to wake up and see that we are the ones responsible for the kids and not vice versa. We have to make the rules and enforce them as hard as it may be.

Just as freedom and responsibility go hand in hand, so do love and responsibility. We can't raise our children in isolation but we can raise them in boundaries. We all have our concepts of right and wrong. We just need to stick to them.

My Mother Still Lives In My heart

A few weeks ago we celebrated Mother's Day. That is a special time when we honor all of the mothers all over the world. It is generally a hard day for me and I guess many, many others whose mothers are not alive.

It is also a hard day I think for my stepmother. She never had any children of her own. And though I love her very much I can never bring myself to call and wish her well on Mother's Day. That is like the last frontier of my heart and one I can not step across.

My mother died when I was 15. My father remarried when I was 16. The wound of my mother's death had not had time to heal before my stepmother came into my life. It was not a particularly happy time for any of us in the family.

My father had known my stepmother all his life. She had been engaged to his younger brother. This younger brother was my father's favorite. He was smart, athletic, bright with promise, and loved by all. But he was destined to have a very short life. In the summer following his graduation from high school he was in a car accident and killed. The bright promise was never fulfilled. The wedding so carefully planned never took place.

In all the years that followed my stepmother never married. She lived in our neighborhood and was loved by us all, but that special someone who could have taken my uncle's place never appeared. But then my mother died and my father needed someone. This time my stepmother did become a "Cooper."

Who knows what goes on in the inner hearts of families. I am sure to outsiders we looked like a very happy family. But we weren't. I resented someone taking my mother's place and I more than disliked my father for letting it happen. It was a war that seethed and raged for years. No one was the winner.

All through high school, college and law school the skirmishes took place. There were truces and violations and more truces. It looked like the war would never end. But it did. It ended with my getting married. And with that event I became a part of my own family and not a contender in theirs.

True happiness for my stepmother and me came when I had children. The woman who could not really be my mother became in all respects a grandmother. My boys loved her and cherished her from the day she first held them. And through their love I began to love her too.

Today we have a great relationship. It is one we have earned. I love her as my father's wife. I love her as my children's grandmother. And I love her as a dear friend. But she still is not my mother and I have begun to realize she never wanted to be.

Still I know on Mother's Day it hurts a little not to be remembered. And maybe if I were a better person I would. But inside my head and inside my heart there is an area of love devoted only to my mother and it burns as brightly now as it did 32 years ago. And she is the one I remember every day and especially on Mother's Day.

Summer Has Its Own Rhythm

Can you believe it has gotten here already? I walked out the door last Saturday and lo and behold it was summer. For some reason I had been thinking it was still spring and summer had "snuck" in. The trees had all bloomed, the ground had gotten dry, and the air had gotten hot. What a great surprise! It's summer!

When I was growing up summer never sneaked up like that. I always knew when it was coming and sometimes I tried to push the season a little. Summer meant freedom from school, and days that went on forever. It was the nearest thing to heaven we could find and it happened every year.

When I was about 7 or 8 years-old my brother and I started our own business one summer. My folks ran a local grocery store and we decided to capitalize on that. So we opened up a "Sno-Jo" stand right outside the door to the store.

Do you all remember what "sno-jo's" were. They were cups of shaved ice, in a cup, with different kinds of flavored drink poured over them. They were wonderful. At least to kids back then they were. Kids today would probably think they were terrible.

Anyway, my brother, who was three years older, got the equipment to shave the ice. My folks sprang for a block of ice to shave. And I assembled the different bottles of flavors to pour over the ice. We were in business.

I have to say we did pretty good for a while. We charged a nickel a cone and would even give you a mixture of drinks for that price. We would pour orange and then grape and then strawberry over the ice, giving the customer a gooey mix of flavors. They loved it and bought with a vengeance.

But soon it got really hot standing behind the stand, so we began to eat our own wares. I don't know how many I consumed but my stomach began to feel bloated and confused. All that orange and grape and strawberry was having a hard time mixing.

As the sun beat down, nausea set in. I made a run for the house and stayed there sick for the next hour or more. My business day was over. Still my practical, non-nauseous brother stayed on and made a hefty profit. After I pitched a fit and screamed my lungs out he even shared some of the money with me.

By the next day we had both lost interest in the "sno-jo" business. We had a little cash and that was all I wanted. I didn't care if I never saw another "sno-jo" again. Besides it was too hot to stand in one place all day. And there was a lot going on in the neighborhood I was missing out on. Plus my brother had gotten a paper route so he had another source of income.

With that monkey off my back I was free to do whatever kids do in the summer – which is everything and nothing. I went swimming, I rode my bike, I hiked in the woods and I ate lots of summer food like hot dogs and hamburgers. I had it all.

Now I am grown-up and summer means just more work days. But that doesn't stop the excitement. It is residue of my childhood. When hot weather comes my heart beats a little faster to the beat of "It's summertime, summertime, sum...sum...summertime."

Marriage Didn't Include Movies

This is a story about real people. The names have been changed but the facts and circumstances are true. It is a love story and I have always been a sucker for romance, so it gives me pleasure to pass it on to you.

It started a couple of years ago. That was when I first met Patty. She is a waitress at a place where I eat irregularly. This is just a place I happen into when I am in the area.

I had been in there several times before and Patty had always waited on me but we had never had a conversation. This day we did. And it was a conversation about movies. I was telling her about one I had seen which was very good and I recommended she go to see it.

"Oh I don't get to the movies," she answered, "I love them, but I never get to go."

"Why not?" I asked, not understanding how anybody could not go to the movies if they loved them as she obviously did.

"Well my husband doesn't like them so we don't go," she explained.

"At least you can rent the videocassettes," I offered, but that too was rejected as her husband didn't think people should waste their time and money on videos. I wondered to myself why he should be able to reject this out of hand since she obviously earned money waiting on tables. But I kept that thought to myself. I try not to interject myself into people's marriages. They seem to have enough trouble without my help.

So I let the conversation end. Still I did notice a trace of sadness about Patty and a note of melancholy in her voice that had to be more than the fact she hadn't seen the latest movies.

The next few times I saw her she asked about the recent movies. I always told her about the ones I had seen and she seemed to enjoy just hearing about them. But the sadness and melancholy I had noticed got more and more pronounced.

One day when Patty came to my table to take my order she asked me for the best movies out on video. When I asked if she had gotten a VCR she offered a quick response.

"I lost a husband and gained a VCR," she told me. "He decided he didn't want to be married anymore and took off with someone younger. So now I don't have anybody to tell me I can't have a VCR."

But even as she told me this, her face began to crumble and she began to fight back tears. I realized that even though he had been a man who didn't like movies, he had also been her husband and the father of her children. And giving someone up could be very hard indeed.

Patty was definitely at a low point in her life. She had three children to raise and she was alone. The ex-husband provided money for the kids, but he didn't see them a lot. He was involved in his new life and wife. Happiness for Patty looked to be a thing of the past.

Each time I saw Patty after that she would tell me about the movies she had rented and how she liked them. She still hadn't started going to see movies in the theaters because her time was taken up with the kids in school and other things. She did say she had dated some but nothing important, and nobody who had taken her to the movies.

But one day when I went to eat she did tell me about a man her brother-in-law had introduced her to. He worked with the airlines and he was from California. I never understood what he was doing in Georgia, but it had something to do with the airport in Atlanta. Anyway he had met Patty and had taken her to the movies.

The next time I saw her was at the movies. It was on a Sunday afternoon. I was in line to get some popcorn and she came in with five children. She spied me in the line and came over to me.

"Say hello to Mr. Cooper," she directed and they all proceeded to shake my hand and say hello. I was impressed as they were all nice looking kids and very well-mannered.

"These aren't all yours are they, Patty?" I asked.

"These three are," she answered, touching the heads of three of them. "And these two soon will be 'cause I am marrying their daddy," she said with a beaming smile. The kids smiled too and miracle of miracles didn't even look embarrassed.

The movies were starting and they had to get food so Patty and I didn't get a chance to talk. But I made sure I went back to her restaurant soon to hear her story.

And the story was that she had fallen in love with the airlines guy, the man who took her to the movies. They had dated for several months and now Patty and her children were going to be moving to California.

When I asked what the kids thought of that she answered that they were tickled to death. "I don't think I could move them out there if they were really against it," she said. "You know I have got to think of their happiness too."

That was just like Patty, always putting everyone else's happiness ahead of hers. But this time it worked out that she could be happy too.

"You would really like him, Mr. Cooper," she said. "He loves the movies. I mean he goes to see at least one a week and maybe more. And he likes videos and everything."

I assured her that I knew I would like him and said I hoped I got to meet him.

Well I didn't get to meet him. And I didn't get to tell Patty good-bye. I found out yesterday that she and the kids are on a train headed for California. Patty and Ben (her new husband's name) got married a couple of weeks ago. Then he flew back to California while she waited for the kids' school to be out. Now they are on their way.

Patty packed them all on the train because she hates to fly. She and I had that in common too. But I think in her heart Patty is really flying. She is headed for happiness and a new life with a man who loves the movies. That doesn't guarantee happiness but it sure gives her a head start.

Feline Offers Felicitous Care

Last week I was hit with that awful, awful illness – the summertime flu. It knocks you down, drags you out, and in general makes your life miserable. All I wanted to do was get home, get in bed and sleep. And basically that is all I did. My wife and children provided me with concern and care but they also wisely just left me alone as much as possible. But not Nurse Sally. She stayed with me through it all.

Nurse Sally came to me on the first day I was home sick. She crept in on little cat's paws and surveyed the situation. "Hmmm, a real sick one here," she thought. "I guess I had better stay here with him and see if he needs anything."

And stay she did. Like glue she stuck to me. At first I didn't recognize her. She looked identical to our cat, Fluff. But we all know that Fluff spends her days in isolation usually by an air vent. She can not be bothered to eat much less give anyone any concern. Eating, attention and affection are reserved for those hours after 6 when she stirs and comes alive for a while.

But this cat who attached herself to my room was an entirely different matter. She wasn't aloof. She would get right in my face and make all kind of noises as if to say, "How are you feeling? Need anything? Well don't worry I am here."

Her hours of duty began around 8:30 each morning when Terry and the boys would start on their activities. I would hear her paws on the stairs and soon she would be loping into my room. She would spring agilely onto the bed, check me out, and then find her spot. There she would stay until 7 or 8 that night.

Terry would bring me soup to eat and Nurse Sally made no effort to join me. She just made mewing sounds of approval. It comforted me to know she thought I was being treated with the right medicine and attention.

Then there was the day I woke up and Nurse Sally was trying to make me look better groomed. All over my head she was going with her tongue trying to get my unruly hair to lay down. I could hear her muttering under her breath, "What if someone came to visit and he looked like this? What would they think of me? And here he is without even a sponge bath. Well, I will take care of that."

Do you know how hard it is to convince a cat to stop licking you once they have made up their mind to do it. I had to really offend Nurse Sally to make her stop. But I just didn't want her cleanliness habits to spill over to me.

Luckily Sally had a forgiving heart and came back to my side after I had rejected her. And there she stayed until I was well, or at least feeling good enough to go back to work.

I am well now and things are back to normal. Nurse Sally has gone and Fluff is back in her place. She gives me some attention but nothing major. I am no longer her concern. But every once in a while I see a gleam in her cat eyes and I expect her to come loping in carrying her degree from med school with her.

I even caught her watching "Today's Health" on television a few days ago, so I think she is brushing up. Maybe getting ready for some specialization work. If she does decide to go back into practice I hope she hangs her shingle out at our house. I know good nurses are hard to find, but so are good cats.

Camp Was A Wash-out

Summertime is the time for going to camp and enjoying nature. That's the way it is now and the way it has always been. It was even that way back in the dark ages when I was a child. Much to my sorrow, that was the way it was then.

Camp was one of the few things my parents made me do. I was able to put it off when I was 7, 8, and 9, but when I turned 10 it could be put off no longer. My friend John Oldham and I were being shipped off together. He was excited about it. I was not.

How could my parents send me away for a week? That was almost an eternity. I could waste away and die during that time, but no amount of pleading could stop the inevitable from happening. It was going to be good for me. John and I would have a great time. They promised me we would.

Being left at camp on that Sunday afternoon was one of the most traumatic events of my life up to that time. All around me were strangers, except for John. Plus, I was suddenly being plunged into nature, a place with which I was not well acquainted. It was little Jackie Cooper versus the wilderness and I was afraid the wilderness would win.

Although I didn't like many sports or camp activities, I did like to swim. So I knew I could pass a lot of the hours by swimming. There was a huge like for that activity as well as canoeing. I was able to keep my sanity with the thought of that fun to hold on to.

The next day I eagerly awaited getting into that lake. Down the hill John and I raced to get in line to swim. But we soon learned there was something called the "buddy system." That meant you swam with a partner at all times, and when the big bell on the dock was chimed you had to hold up your buddy's hand.

John and I were buddies. But to get to swim we had to pass the swimming test. That meant swimming out to a raft and back. It was a piece of cake for me, but not for John. He didn't make it out there and back. The lifeguard had to go in and get him. That meant no swimming in the lake for him. He could only play in the shallow part, or the "baby pond" as the other campers called it.

My mind immediately began to plot to find another more capable swimmer to buddy with. But as soon as I said anything about it, John began to beg me not to leave him. I now had an albatross about my neck the size of a healthy 10 year-old, and it was pulling me under.

The rest of the week was a blur of tears and ping pong. I cried myself to sleep at night. I cried during the rest time in the afternoon. I teared up during meals and during the evening campfire. I was one soggy camper. But John was happy. He loved to play ping pong, and that is what we did.

Day in and day out when there was any free time we played ping pong. I became an expert. If there had been a Wimbledon for ping pong expertise, I would have been seeded first. And John would have been right behind.

Of course I did survive the week. My parents came on Sunday and took me home. I eventually forgave them. But I never went back to camp until years later when I was in college. Then I went back to this same camp as a counselor. Was I a good counselor? You had better believe it. I was determined no kid would have as rotten a week as the one I had suffered through when I was 10.

Stage Set For 'Methodist Miracle'

To get the full impact of this story you must recognize two facts. These facts about me and my family will set the stage for an occurrence of monumental proportions which occurred last Sunday. But before I tell you about that, let's get the facts straight.

Number one – my father used to be a Merita Bread salesman. He was a company man and he lived and breathed Merita Bread and everything connected with it. One of the most important aspects of bread selling was that Merita sponsored the TV show "The Lone Ranger." So this masked man became one of my father's heroes and almost a member of the family. It would not have surprised me for "Uncle Lone and/or Cousin Tonto" to come riding up to our house in Clinton at any time.

All through my childhood I was a member of "The Lone Ranger Fan Club" and so, I expect, was my Dad. I do know the last and just about only movie my father ever saw was the movie "The Lone Ranger and the Seven Cities of Gold." For that one he gathered us all up, took us downtown, and bought four tickets. Talk about monumental events, that really was one.

Number two – my father and stepmother are dyed-in-the-wool Baptists, always have been and always will be. I, on the other hand, have been a Methodist for the last 16 years. Even though I married a good Baptist girl, she and I jointly decided to transfer to the Methodist faith.

Now my folks know I would never have taken such a step on my own so I must have had my own Eve to tempt me to the other denomination. They cannot accept the fact that it was I who lured her to membership in a non-baptizing church.

Year end and year out I have heard the same complaints from them, after they visited in my Methodist church. One is that the church never recognizes visitors. Every time we went to church I would pray someone would say a welcome to them. I even lined people up to come and say hello. But they never felt overwhelmed by greetings.

Now in their Baptist church the preacher has everyone sign a card and then he reads the names of visitors from the pulpit. That is the way they think it should be done. But even if my preacher wouldn't do that, they complained, he should at least recognize visitors in some way.

Strike one was not being recognized as a "visitor" by the preacher. Strike two was not having the congregation say hello. Strike three was not having an open altar call.

My folks could not understand a church service where the heathens were not invited to come forward and lay aside their sins and join the fold. How were we to save the world if that was not done! Why didn't my Methodist church do it!

I had no answers. I tired of the debate. I became more firmly entrenched in the Methodist church than ever before. Right or wrong it was my church and I loved it and I was going to stay there. But still in my mind I hoped that something would happen that would give my parents' peace of mind and acceptance of my family being Methodist.

The power of prayer has always been one of my strong suits, and I did pray about this matter of my parents' anxiety over and over. Last Sunday my prayers were answered. The new preacher we had gotten in the last turn over of the Methodist pastor assignments brought it about. He was God's instrument in this crucial area of my life and probably didn't even know he was being used.

My parents were visiting us last weekend to celebrate my father's birthday. On Sunday we went to church and I knew over lunch there would be the same negative comments. Anyway, we had just gotten to our seats at 9 a.m. service when the minister asked that all the visitors stand. Up my parents popped, and glory hallelujah I silently shouted! We were then all invited to greet those who were visiting and millions of people said "hello" and "how are you" to the older couple from Clinton, SC. My cup runneth over.

Then before we were seated we all sang one verse of "Bless Be the Tie That Binds." Now all denominations claim this song, but I knew my folks were thinking in their minds that we were singing a good Baptist song. They sang out with gusto. And so did I.

I thought that was enough of a blessing for one day but God had more in store for me. When we got to the sermon the preacher talked about heroes. And one of the heroes he discussed was – you've got it – the Lone Ranger. I could see my Daddy beaming. His faith had been vindicated. He and the preacher knew the Lone Ranger was a worthy hero.

If you think it stopped here, you have got to read on. As the icing on the cake we got one more surprise. Before we had heard the benediction the pastor gave an altar call. It was a complete shock to me but I was so grateful I felt like going forward myself.

God, the preacher, and I had gone for the gold and scored a perfect 10. On the Sunday my father turned 75 years old he could finally relax and not worry about my Methodist salvation. It really was going to be all right.

My folks are still Baptist. Last Sunday did not convert them to the Methodist faith. But I think it did open their eyes a little and teach them some tolerance and understanding. I hope so because I really do want to be compatible with my parents in all things. But I am Methodist now. For whatever reasons it is the way I have chosen. I have always had God's blessing and as of last Sunday, thank God, I have my parents too.

Faithful Automobile Retired

Four years ago I bought a little red compact car that I used on my travels around the state and to go to and from work. It suited my needs and got me everywhere I had to be. Over the course of the four years it came to be one of my very best friends. Just like a character from a children's story I always thought of it as "the little red car."

This past weekend I traded in "the little red car" on a big silver car. I drove my little friend to South Carolina and left her with my cousin, the car dealer. It was not easy saying goodbye to such a faithful companion.

When we left home on Saturday morning to drive the 200 miles to the dealership the little red car had 122,000 miles on her odometer. That is 122,000 big ones. This little car was not as young as she once was and none of her parts were in great shape.

Still she bravely let me load her up with my wife and two big sons for the trip. They were a little cramped and my wife was a little anxious that the car wouldn't make it there. But I knew she would. Just like the little train in the children's story, I could hear the little red car saying, "I think I can! I think I can!" all the way to South Carolina.

On the way there I thought back to the times we had had together. The car had never let me down even though I had not treated her the best. I would forget about oil changes and getting her washed. I let her seats spring holes and never got them repaired. I just stuffed a pillow onto the seat and let that keep the springs from tearing the back of my pants.

I hate to say it but towards the end I became ashamed to be seen with her. Even though I had been responsible for her loss of shine and sparkle, I blamed her for her dumpy body and messy interior. I felt that at this point in time and at my age I deserved something better.

It was not an easy decision to make. For some reason I hate to buy cars. I would rather drive the wheels off one than go through the hassle of dealing with car dealers. But my cousin came through with an offer I couldn't refuse and so the little red car had to go.

You will never convince me that inanimate objects don't take on a personality over the years. I know this car did. It loved me as much as a car could love a human. It never ran out of gas even though we rode sometimes on fumes. And if it was going to break down it did so within walking distance of a garage. I never feared when I was on the interstate because I knew the car would get me safely to a town before overheating or anything of that nature.

When I left in my shiny silver car I looked back in the rearview mirror at the little red car. Some would say that was only air conditioner moisture coming out of her, but I know it was tears. You'll never convince me otherwise.

All during those 122,000 miles the heart of the little red car said "I think I can! I think I can!" Now I just hope she can find someone else to appreciate her and give her peace in her older days – "I hope she can! I hope she can!"

But Can She Deliver Pups?

For some unknown reason it crossed my mind the other day to wonder what the girls my sons marry will be like. I hope it is somebody I like. Other than that it can be their own choices. My wife tells me that she prays daily for the women who are going to be our daughters someday. That is a good thing to do and helps relieve the old mind at the same time.

I, of course, would love to see them bring home someone as wonderful as their mother. Then the three couples could spend the rest of their lives in harmony and joy with grandchildren in abundance surrounding our feet. I am sure it will work out just that way – ha, ha, ha.

When I was growing up I always had two criteria for the woman I was going to marry. Number one, she had to be a cheerleader. And number two, she had to know how to deliver puppies. There was a logic to it but it looks pretty shallow now.

First off there just was and is something bouncy and bright about girls who are cheerleaders. They seem to embody the all American spirit and zest for life. I never met a cheerleader who wasn't full of excitement or one who didn't seem to be happy to be alive.

Secondly, we had dogs when I was growing up and it used to amaze me that my mother who had no medical training could deliver puppies. It was like she had the secret of life.

Okay, I was pretty young when I first thought this but it stuck with me.

In high school I did start going with Elaine, the cheerleader. And she was bright, bouncy and enthusiastic. She was also two years younger than I which must have been the reason she didn't bop me up the side of the head when I asked if she could deliver puppies. Instead she just got real serious and said she could always learn.

Well as far as I know Elaine never did learn to deliver puppies. Instead she married a peanut butter salesman and raised two kids. Obviously his criteria was not the same as mine. But then my criteria also changed.

My wife was not a cheerleader, nor has she ever delivered a litter of puppies. She is however the kind of person who could do anything she set her mind to. But if I had asked her something stupid like could she deliver puppies she would have told me to take a hike. She does not suffer fools easily.

The point of all this is cheerleading and puppy delivery are not things upon which to base character. Thankfully my sons seem to have a better grasp on life than I did at their ages and know there are traits of much more importance. Still there is an exuberance for life cheerleaders exude that can't really be faked. And having the ability to aid in the beginning of life has to be something extra in a person's makeup.

So my criteria may not be logical for the top two requirements in a spouse but I still think they could be in anyone's top ten. Ladies, your rebuttals to these comments are welcome.

Money Can't Buy It All

Sometimes when I am thinking deep thoughts I realize they have come from my Sunday School lesson for the week. You would be surprised at the topics that are located there. For example, this week we are studying "Family Stress" and the specific topic is "Materialism." Now there's something that affects everyone. We either have too much or too little of the material things.

It is understandable that my parents' generation was materialistic for they had suffered through the depression and knew what a real lack of the necessities was. My father always laughs when people talk about the good old days. "Don't give me the good old days," he says, "I'll take the present any day."

Still I have always been aware that my parents' ideas of success meant money. When talking about people with whom I graduated high school, they will say that he/she is making "big money" or they live in a "fine" home. I never know exactly how much "big money" is, or how fine a "fine" home is. I guess it is all in the eyes of the beholder.

The funny thing is that people of my generation are so materialistic. Most of my contemporaries were raised in middle class abundance. They didn't really have to do without the necessities although they may not have had EVERYTHING they wanted. But today they are determined to have all the goodies of life that they can grab.

A few years ago my wife and I decided to build our dream house. We got a good builder and some great plans and started into the project. It became the most important thing in our lives. We ate, drank, and dreamed house. We talked about it from sun-up to sun-down and expected everyone to share our enthusiasm.

A few months before the house was to be completed we had an illness in our family. For a short period of time things looked bad. At that point in time the house and all of the pleasure it promised went out the window. We didn't care two hoots for house, all we wanted was health.

Thank God everything with the health problem was solved, and we went back to normal living. But we didn't forget how insignificant the house had become at that time. We still looked forward to moving into it but we didn't see it as the end-all to happiness.

I still remember the feeling I had when I thought there was a problem that money could not solve. All the money in the world cannot buy the solution to sickness, emotional distress, and other related occurrences. Oh, it can help. I admit that. But money alone cannot buy happiness.

Despite my Baptist upbringing I do not believe that wealth equates to sin. Nor do I believe that poverty makes us saints. But I do believe we have to have our priorities in the right place and that is where the problems come in.

We owe it to ourselves and our children to keep things in perspective. If we raise a generation of kids to believe that money and material things are the end-all, then we have served them badly. I want my children to live the good life but I also want them to know what "goodness" really is.

Now even if you don't go to Sunday School, you have had your lesson.

Cats Can Be Jailbirds Too

She is home now. After a week in a caged cell she is a free woman. Her only offense was a minor one but it got her locked up for five days. I never thought I would have someone in my own family locked up like that but I had to do it. It was the only way to keep the peace.

It all started a few weeks ago when we learned my in-laws were going to pay us a five-day visit. They had not been to see us for a while so we were anxious to see them. But we also knew we had a problem. My wife's mother has allergies and one thing that sets her off good is cat hair. And we have a cat.

We asked Fluff if she could quit shedding for a few days but she couldn't make any promises. It is just second nature with her and something she can't control. She said she would try but that just wasn't good enough.

After much discussion it was decided Fluff would have to spend the time they were here at the vet's. It was a hard decision to make but we had no choice. So on Tuesday we bundled her up with one of JJ's old shirts for company and took her in. You would have thought we were sending her up the river. I never ever saw a cat look so sad.

On Wednesday when I got home and was checking the messages on our answer machine there was one of pleading meows. I guess they gave her one call before they locked her up. It really broke my heart to hear her pleading like that but I couldn't give in. She had to serve the full sentence.

On Saturday when we went to get her it was quite a shock. She came out with a swagger and a cigarette hanging out of her mouth. She had gone from being a timid housecat to a hardened and felonious feline. She had had to get tough to make it so get tough she did.

All the way home she was cool and casual to us. She appeared annoyed when we tried to scratch her back or between her eyes, usually two of her favorite places. She seemed to be more of a "Flo" than a "Fluff." That's what she said the other cool cats at the big house called her.

When we got to the house she seemed surprised there were no bars on the windows. She went about sniffing out her old hangouts. But still she remained hostile and surly.

It wasn't until a couple of days later that the old "Fluff" returned. I was sitting on the couch and she jumped up on the back of it and began to lick my head. That was the first sign that all was forgiven.

I don't know what we will do the next time my in-laws come to town. I have promised Fluff we won't send her away like that again. But I may not have to worry. By then she may have a new career as a country music queen. I heard her in her room the other night playing her guitar and singing a song she wrote about her experience. It is called "My In-laws Made an Outlaw Out of Me."

Reba and Dolly have called about using it on their next albums. It sounds like a hit. Maybe some good came out of the experience after all.

Time Flies By When You're Having Fun

It has happened again. Yesterday was the first of June and today is the end of August. The summer started and ended in the blink of an eye. All of those vacations, projects, adventures, and experiences I planned for the three months of summer never materialized. The days just slipped into months and then it was all gone.

How does time change its pace? I just don't understand it. If three months of summer vacation was a long time in my teens, why isn't it the same today? Twenty-four hours should be 24 hours regardless of your age.

But it does go fast, and it did go fast, and now my sons are starting school again. This will be my oldest son's senior year and already my wife and I have started the "last time" song. This was the last time we would register him in high school, and on and on and on.

A senior in high school! Do you remember that time in your life? I think that was one of the greatest feelings in the world. At that point in time you really were king of the mountain. I didn't feel it when I was a senior in college. Then there was too much fear of starting out in the real world and having to face reality. But in high school there was still the buffer of college coming up so you could relax and enjoy the year to the fullest.

When I was a senior we had special days that sound so trivial now, but back then they were important. One was called "Senior Barefoot Day." On that day we all got to go to school barefoot – seniors that is. And everyone did it. Even the prissiest girls walked around with dirty feet for an entire day.

The girls of course had a great time painting their toenails special colors and making them attractive. The boys stuck with bare feet unless you had a special girl and then you wrote her name in paint of some type across the top of your foot. Now there is a show of true love.

Aside from "barefoot day" there was also the senior treat of leading into chapel and leading out. No one sat down until the seniors had entered the auditorium and no one left until the seniors were on their way out. We also were first into the lunchroom and first out of there. And on some days there were senior specials – food served only to seniors.

To be truthful we as a senior class didn't spend too much time in the lunchroom. We were always outside at the coke machines with a bag of popcorn to finish our meal. I wonder how we ever grew up healthy on that rigid diet. The dumb thing was we were always hungry but we still only ate popcorn and drank cokes.

That was too many years ago to be counted, but that feeling of being a special senior still lingers. It is one of those feelings and memories you keep with you all your life. Whoever thought it up should be in the hall of fame.

And whoever it was who wrote the song "Sunrise, Sunset" should be in there too. As I look at my children growing up before my eyes I can hear the words of that song in my head. Their growing up does happen almost overnight, and with one sunrise and sunset the days do fly too quickly by.

Get Out Of Abuse-filled Relationship

A few days ago I was watching a program on television about battered wives. It amazed me that so many women are the victims of physical abuse from their spouses. You would think that in this day and age of so called enlightenment such cruelty would be a thing of the past. But this show quoted statistics saying every 15 seconds a woman in America is abused by her spouse or partner.

In the show I watched the women interviewed ranged from military officer's wife to oil company executive, from secretary to social worker, and from 20 years-old to 50 years-old. There was no one stereotypical abused woman and there was no one stereotypical abusing male.

When I was in college I had a friend named Marty. He was a good guy from a good family. He was smart, sociable and well liked. In our sophomore year he started dating a girl named Theresa. She was also cute, intelligent and well liked. They appeared to be one of those perfect couples that meet up in college and have a long and happy life together.

One night after Marty and Theresa had been out on a date, Marty came to my room. He was upset because he and Theresa had had an argument and he had ended up hitting her.

"I couldn't help myself, Jackie," he said. "I was trying to get her to act right and she said something smart so I smacked her."

I was shocked. I had never known anybody who smacked their girlfriend around. But Marty seemed to be contrite and said he would never do it again. I kind of just let it drop and so did he. But then I heard him telling some other guys about it and they were saying good for him. They seemed to think Theresa had probably deserved it.

Many, many times after that Marty would tell me again how he had had to smack Theresa around a little bit to make her understand his point on something. And more than once I saw bruises on Theresa. But she kept dating him and I kept thinking it was none of my business.

After our sophomore year Theresa did not come back to my college and Marty transferred to another one. The last I heard about him he was on his third marriage. I don't know what happened to Theresa.

The point of this is that "nice" people can be involved in this type of activity. Men can find a macho image in beating up their wife and/or kids. And wives can feel so worthless that they think they deserve to be beaten.

The sad thing is that abused children tend to grow up to be abusing parents. A young boy who sees his father abuse his mother may hate it when it is happening, and yet that same young man may very well grow up to be a person who abuses his wife. It is a vicious cycle.

With our society becoming more and more a violent one, people are constantly looking for reasons why. A lot has to do with the way we are conditioned to accept violence. We allow small children to watch violence in films and on television and then expect them to be nonviolent people. It just doesn't work that way.

We as individuals have to realize that violence begets violence. And exposure to violent acts numbs us to the horror of it. Plus we have to teach our children and our selves that being abusive is not being manly, and being submissive to violence is not being feminine. The time for those roles to be abandoned is long since past.

To Pray Or Not To Pray Is A Big Issue

This issue of school prayer is getting completely out of hand. I just don't see why it can't be handled by majority rule. If a majority of the people involved in an event such as a football game want to start the game with prayer, why can't they. No one should be forced to participate but I don't think the dissenters should be able to void the rights of others.

When the founding fathers talked about separation of church and state I don't think they meant for it to be carried to these extremes. Just think how far we could take this issue if we wanted to. When a person sneezes we might only be able to have a moment of silence instead of saying "God bless you!"

Prayer has always been a part of my life. It was something I learned at home. My parents always had bedtime prayers with us and we took turns praying. I always liked it when it was my Daddy's turn because his were the shortest. My brother was so good that he always drew his out, and mine were brief but awkward.

My mother always prayed the longest prayers. She covered all the events of the day that had just ended and also anything that was coming up during the next day. But I could always tell when she was getting towards the end of her prayers for that was when she blessed "the poor, the sick and the unfortunate." It was like her special signal to God that all was okay and it also served as a reassurance to me.

Years later when I used to watch Carol Burnett pull her ear as a secret sign to her family, I would think about "the poor, the sick and the unfortunate." That phrase from my mother's prayer was just as unique to her as Carol's ear pulling was to her family.

Yes prayer has always been a part of my family history. It is legend that years ago my aunt was called upon to pray in church. Now this was back when women usually were quiet in the order of service, but maybe this preacher was very forward thinking or something of that nature.

Anyway my aunt was and is a very formal lady. She always does the right thing, and heaven help her children if they didn't. So on this night of the prayer she rose out of her seat and stood very erect.

"Let us bow our heads in prayer," she said. And all heads bowed in unison.

Then she proceeded in her most authoritative voice, "God is great, God is good. Let us thank him for everything. By His hand we all are fed. He gives to us everything. Amen."

Children were falling in the aisles and adults were biting back laughs. My aunt, the most formal lady in the world, had just led the congregation in prayer by saying a child's meal blessing. But no one said a word to her. Not a sound of criticism was heard. She had pulled it off.

And you know I bet God thought it was a pretty good prayer. As long as we say what is in our hearts, be it silent or aloud, it gets the message across.

I don't want to force my religion on anyone, and I don't want to their beliefs to be forced on me. As long as no one is forced to participate in what the majority wants to do, then I think it should be allowed. Freedom is a double edged sword. It says you can do or not do what your heart and mind dictate.

Birthdays Aren't Memorable

Yes, another year has come and passed. As of last Wednesday I am another year older. Funny how they seem to come by faster and faster as I get older and older.. But this year I did get through the day without getting suicidal, or even suffering a moderate depression.

The fact that it is my birthday is not what usually sends me into the depths of despair, it is just the fact it is a special day like a holiday. And I generally get down on holidays. But not this year. This year I was in good shape. I willed myself not to get in a blue mood.

People who know how I am on holidays and birthdays generally do not understand. That is OK. I don't understand it either. It is something that just happens. The best thing for me to do is just try to go about my normal routine and forget the occasion.

My wife thinks no one should have to work on their birthday. It should be a free day from all the normal demands of life and work. Not me. I want to keep to my normal routine as much as possible. A little piece of cake is okay but no party and no crowd of friends around.

When I was a little boy my family used to ask what I wanted for my birthday and usually the answer was nothing. I could always think of something to buy during the other 365 days but on my birthday I really didn't want anything extra.

I do remember one time my mother took me uptown on my birthday. It was a Saturday and she said we would do anything I wanted to do. My father was working and my brother was visiting with some friends so it was just me and her.

First off we went to the local drugstore, where they also had a soda and fountain part, and ordered ham sandwiches and chocolate milkshakes. The sandwiches here were always toasted just right and had the best dill pickle slices on top that could not be found anywhere else. Plus the milkshakes were good and lumpy like they were supposed to be.

Afterwards I wanted to go to the movies – what else. We only had one theater in town so we didn't have much of a choice as to what we were going to see. It turned out we saw a western entitled "Salome Where She Danced." You haven't seen it? What a pity! It was a real classic starring Yvonne DeCarlo.

For some reason that is my favorite birthday memory. Not a lot of great presents, not a big cake with ice cream, not even a party with a lot of friends. It was just ham sandwiches, chocolate milkshakes and a movie. Nothing too much out of the ordinary but on that day and at that time it was everything I wanted it to be.

I don't know if my children will or have ever had a special day like that one was for me. I am sure they would die if I asked them to go out for sandwiches and then a movie. That is not their idea of a treat. We are all different and what pleases one will not please another. But I hope I have given them some days like this one that will live in their memories forever.

You Can't Believe Everything

Years ago there was a song titled "How Could You Believe Me When I Said I Loved You When You Know I've Been A Liar All My Life?" When I first heard it I didn't get the impact of what it meant. Later I learned it meant that if you believe everything you hear you are one gullible fool. And that has been a problem with me all my life.

I basically want to trust people. That should be simple enough but it isn't. The truth is that people lie, and that they do it more often than not. I try to teach my children to be trusting but I also have to temper that with "but don't believe everything you hear." It is a sad world we live in when a person's word is only as good as the convenience of the truth.

My gullibility started in high school. Well, it was probably before that but my first recollections were from high school. My two friends Hollis and Chuck knew I would believe anything and they would make up the wildest tales just to see how hard I would fall for them. It was like Charlie Brown and Lucy. He always knows she is going to take away the football before he kicks it, but she is always able to talk him into trying one more time.

Initially Hollis and Chuck would tell me simple lies, like the wrong time for the movie to start. Then they graduated to bigger plots like the time they told me it was "Senior Dress Up Day." Just about everyone was in on that one. I showed up in coat and tie. The only person at the school in a coat and tie!

This gullibility condition has persisted. When I was in the military I was in investigations. Another guy and myself were investigating a theft of funds. It came down to one person being under suspicion. Don, the other investigator, and I interrogated the man. He said he was innocent. I believed him. Don did not.

I went back and talked with him on my own. He swore to me he had not taken the money. He told me he was going to be a preacher when he got out of service. He swore on his smallest child's head he wasn't lying. I believed him! I believed him! I believed him!

Don kept telling me the evidence against him was too great. But I just as stubbornly told him of my gut feeling. I would be the great defender. I would prove the innocence of this accused man.

I was at home working on my letter to the base commander putting my neck on the line for this guy when I got a call. Don said I needed to come down and get a statement. I said I was too busy. He said if I took this statement I wouldn't be so busy – the guy had just confessed.

So on I go, wanting to believe what everyone tells me and finding that the world is not a place of unvarnished truth.

We are not a totally truthful society. We tell the truth generally when it suits our purposes. And for gullible people like me it is a game of hook, line and sinker.

Sometimes the people we trust the most hurt us the most. Then we make our shells a little tougher and move back into the game. But gullible people generally stay gullible. Trust is something we are born with and it takes a lot of hits to beat it down. When I get hurt I generally swear the only people I will ever trust again are my immediate family. But it doesn't last.

But what do we tell our children? Do we make them

suspicious of everything they are told? Or do we say run the risk and trust? This time I am only phrasing the questions because I sure don't know the answers.

Wasp Mounted As A Trophy

The men in the Cooper family have never been hunters. Some have been fisherman but none to my knowledge has ever indulged in the macho pastime of hunting. I know I have never hunted. Never ever wanted to go out into the woods with gun in hand and stalk down the dreaded, vicious deer that roam about inflicting damage to the countryside and the people who live there.

Still inside even the most tender-hearted male there lurks the "John Wayne" syndrome. For anyone raised on a steady diet of John Wayne westerns the desire to emulate him in some way is always there beneath the surface waiting for a chance to burst forth. Well after all these years it happened to me the other night.

It was well after midnight and all of my family was asleep. I was on the final chapters of the new Stephen King book and I wasn't about to go to bed before I finished it. Even if I had gone to bed the images of King creatures would have haunted my dreams. So on I read, searching for that final solution King gives his tales.

So intent was I on my reading I barely noticed the daredevil wasp that swooped toward my head. Barely missing my nose this stinging creature fairly cackled as he saw me jerk back in shock. He came to a screeching halt in midair and turned for another run at me. One which only my super-sharp reflexes allowed me to avoid.

Looking eye-to-eyes at the wasp I realized it was him or me. Or worse he could fly up the stairs and sting my wife and children while they slept. I knew I couldn't let that happen. I had to be the man of the house and I had to kill that wasp.

But what could I use to slay him. I didn't want to get in too close and run the risk of being stung myself. No, I needed a long distance weapon. I immediately went to the cupboard under the sink to see if we had any bug spray. We didn't. But we did have some "Glass Plus."

Why not, I wondered. I could spray him to death with that as good as anything else. So I pulled out the container and let the wasp have a spray right up the side of his little buggy head. "Hah!" I could hear him cry. "I eat 'Glass Plus' for breakfast." And so it seemed he did for the liquid did not faze him, only made him look madder – and cleaner.

He attacked again and again as I rushed back to the shelf containing the cleaning material. I reached blindly and grabbed another container. This one was "409." I liked the feel of the bottle in my hand and the way it had a trigger to execute the action.

Holding it I was John Wayne in "Rio Bravo" or Gary Cooper in "High Noon." If I had had a belt on I would have strapped it to my hip and marched into battle. Instead I stood back and took deadly aim at the wasp. I pulled the trigger with glee – and nothing happened. Was I out of bullets, I mean spray, I wondered. Nothing that complex, I merely hadn't turned the nozzle and made my weapon ready.

Now I was prepared and I let off a round. It hit the varmint in mid flight. I was dead on target and the wasp was out of luck. I sprayed him twice more and each time my aim was better. He fell to the kitchen table clutching his insect chest, gave a slight wheeze and expired.

I wiped the extra liquid from the squirter and then replaced the bottle on the shelf. The deed was done. I had saved the family. John and Gary would be proud. Maybe even Stephen King would be too.

I probably swaggered a little as I went up the stairs to bed that night. Now I knew a little of what the hunters feel. I still didn't and don't want to be a hunter. But if you look closely in my office, beside the computer screen there is a little trophy on my wall. The head of the wasp has been mounted to show the world they don't mess with "Big Jack," the deadliest shot with "409" you'll ever know.

Some Will Believe Anything

When I was growing up one of my favorite pastimes was listening to my mother tell me local legends and ghost stories. She could really churn them out and I believed them all – hook, line and sinker. If my mother told it then it must be true.

One of her favorites was the headless man who went up and down that railroad tracks looking for the head he lost when the train ran over him. On cloudy nights if you looked real hard you could see the vague light of his lantern moving on the tracks that ran a few blocks from our house.

My favorite was the one she called "The Last Autograph." It concerned a young woman who lived in Clinton. Her name was Alice Jane Sanders. Alice Jane (everyone had two names in those days) was a very pretty girl. She had been raised by doting parents who thought she was truly God's gift from Heaven.

Alice Jane was an only child and was more than a little spoiled. But not in the worst way. She was just a little willful, just a little headstrong. And she loved the spotlight. She gained celebrity in our area by winning beauty contests. She was "Miss This" and "Miss That" and she loved it. And people loved her.

One of the things Alice Jane loved most about her celebrity was signing autographs. The local kids would always approach her when she was out and ask her to sign a napkin or other piece of paper. And Alice Jane would always comply with her trademark signature, a collection of letters written with a sweep and flourish. It was very distinctive.

To keep his baby girl happy Alice Jane's father gave her a brand new convertible to drive around the state to the various pageants. Alice Jane loved that car and she loved to drive it fast. More than once she collected tickets for speeding, but that didn't seem to slow her down. She would act contrite, usually using her charms to get the ticket reduced to a warning, and would be on her way again.

But one night her charms were not enough to prevent harm. Alice Jane rounded a corner at a high speed and flipped her car. Her neck was broken, but her beautiful face was untouched.

Crowds came for her funeral. The coffin was open and the mourners of all ages filed by to say good-bye. No one could believe the vivacious Alice Jane was actually gone. But she was. Death had come early for a young girl who had so much to live for.

Even after a week crowds still came to the cemetery to mourn their loss. Flowers were placed by her tombstone, as were other items of love. Some little girls even left their dolls at the headstone. It was as if people could not bear to give up this young woman who had meant so much to them.

One night there was a tremendous storm and the next morning when mourners went to the cemetery they found the tombstone on Alice Jane's grave had been changed. The dates were still the same but the listing of her name was now spelled out in the flourishing handwriting that had been so identifiable to her. Alice Jane had returned for a brief instant and left a final autograph.

That's the way my mother told the story. I guess she elaborated on some of the details. Because people can't and don't come back – do they? But one thing is sure. If you go to Alice Jane's grave today you will see the gravestone with the dead girl's signature. I know. I have seen it.

There's A Light To Guide Us

Christmas is one of the most hectic times of the year. No matter how busy I am the 11 other months, when December comes I get busier. This sends me into Christmas feeling angry, frustrated, and overcome by it all. So much for Christmas cheer.

This was exactly my mood a few days ago as I drove to Fayetteville, Georgia for an interview with Dr. Ferrol Sams. He is the author of *Whisper of the River, Run With the Horsemen* and *Christmas Gift!* I had long wanted to meet and talk with him so a trip to Fayetteville didn't seem to high a price to pay.

The only problem was I had never been to Fayetteville, and I am lousy at directions. What should have been a trip of only an hour and a half stretched into two. I was only a few minutes late but that was because I had allowed myself some leeway.

When I was leaving Dr. Sams' office I determined I was going to take all the right roads home. And since it was a rainy, dark night in Georgia I was more than ready to be home and out of the elements.

The journey started off good. I made it to Griffin without a hitch. But there I somehow took a wrong turn. Into the backwoods of Georgia I plunged. My car passed through mile after mile of deserted country living. And after an hour or more of driving I ended up 10 miles away from Fayetteville.

I couldn't believe it. I was furious. The song kept going through my mind, "Well did he ever return, no he never returned. And his fate is still unlearned. He may ride forever through the roads of Georgia. He's the man who never returned."

If my wife had been with me I know she would have been saying, "Stop and ask somebody." But the places that had lights didn't look like the places where I wanted to stop. So on I drove.

If you have ever been worried about overpopulation, don't be. There are whole areas out there where nobody lives. It is just fields and woods and winding roads. I know. I have been there.

Just let me find the interstate I prayed, but nothing appeared that looked like a lighted highway. Of course my mind also kept praying that my trusty car would not break down or the tires go flat. And like a champ it didn't. I was safe and warm inside the capsule of my car while the rain and wind howled on the outside.

Eventually my aggravation subsided and I began to enjoy the trip. I had the radio on and there were Christmas songs being played. Plus I had a bag of M&M's I had been saving for a rainy day that I opened and devoured. All and all it wasn't such a bad time after all.

Suddenly I saw a bright light up ahead. I couldn't quite make it out but it was clear enough for me to head towards. When I got closer I discovered it was a tree which some children had decorated with Christmas lights – all white ones. I say children decorated it because there was no pattern to the arrangement of the lights.

Still the glow illuminated the night and it was magnified by a pond in front of the tree. The reflection made the tree seem twice as pretty. I have always liked the word "serendipity" but never knew its true meaning until this unexpected surprise came my way.

I passed by the tree and just a short distance beyond it was the interstate. I actually turned on to it with reluctance. There would be no "unexpected surprises" to inspire me there.

When I got home I thought back about that tree. I don't know if I would be able to find it again if I looked. But I certainly won't forget it. For that Christmas tree personified the message of the season – at Christmastime the brightest light in the world can pierce the darkness and lead us on to the road we are seeking.

Chapter 3

Sad Movies Make Me Cry

I know it is not the manly thing to say but it is the truth nonetheless, sad movies make me cry! It is true now and it was true from the very start. If you put me in a darkened theater and throw something on the screen to touch the heart, well you can count on me to tear up.

Now I am not as bad as my college buddy Gordon Johnson. He was the most tender-hearted person I have ever known. Every time we went to the movies during those college years Gordon would find something in the film to shed some tears over. Now don't think this was because he was weak. It wasn't. Gordon played basketball and was one of the stars of the team. He just had a soft spot for things sentimental or sad and he let it come out in tears.

My clearest moment of Gordon and his tender streak came when we went to see a re-release of "Old Yeller." The opening credits started and so did Gordon. All through the film he sniffed and wheezed. Then when the kid had to shoot the dog Gordon lost it. He almost flooded the theater. We swore him off dog movies from that day forward.

"E.T." gave me my worst tear times. My wife and I were living in California at the time of its release. I had been invited to a pre-release screening in Hollywood. It was being screened at the Academy Award Theater in Beverly Hills and the audience was sprinkled with real celebrities. Goldie Hawn, Elliot Gould and Donald Sutherland were just a few of those there.

The audience was packed and we were lucky to get two good seats. It was strange there was such a crowd because at that time Speilberg was not such a big name and there had really been little advance hype about the film. But everyone suspected something major was going to be seen that night.

My wife and I were seated on a side row next to a couple we did not know. Somehow I ended up seated next to the unknown wife with my wife on my right and the lady's husband on her left. She had wisely brought a box of Kleenex with her.

The lights dimmed and the movie started. As the saga of the little alien creature was told my eyes began to mist over. My wife gave me a nudge at the first snort. From there it went from bad to worse. The lady on my right was in even worse shape. Her husband was turned completely away from her and she was sobbing her heart out. I soon joined her.

We became instant allies in that theater and we shared that box of Kleenex like there was no tomorrow. We would watch the screen, look at each other, and cry. If ever two people needed each other it was us.

When the movie ended we straightened up and cleaned up our act. I don't think we ever even spoke. She left with her husband and I left with my wife. Crying time was over. But I will never ever forget her and the tissues we shared.

Since that time I have seen a few more tear jerkers. I can never predict which ones will make me cry. I do know that in "Gone With The Wind" I am gone from the time Bonnie dies till the last scene where Rhett doesn't give a damn. And I also know that any movie with an animal dying will tear me up.

Otherwise I may or may not react. Sometimes I look around at people sniffing during certain scenes and wonder what they are seeing that I am missing. I guess we all relate to things from a personal experience and what may touch one will leave another cold. But I don't think tears are bad for anyone. It is a good catharsis for men, women or children.

So if tears in a theater embarrass you, don't take a seat near me. If it hits my heart in the right way then they are going to flow – and from my point of view the sadder the better.

Turn Around And They're Grown

Last week we started the first official step of the long journey of college. Yes, it has happened. Our oldest son is getting ready to enter college in the fall. Now where the time went to since he was 6, I don't know. I keep thinking I will wake up and my boys will be 3 and 6 again and all this grown-up stuff will have been a bad dream. But I don't think that it is going to happen.

Anyway last week was the time to go to the University of Georgia for orientation. I was really flattered our son wanted his parents to go. I remember when I was ready to go off and look at colleges I did it with a couple of friends – no parents were in my plan. But our son said OK so off we went, with him.

We left home around six in the morning and made the two-hour drive. It was like a surrealistic scene from a movie. There was fog everywhere as we drove across the backroads of Georgia and the car just seemed to glide through the mist. It was the perfect setting for the conflicting thoughts which were going through my mind.

Once we arrived we were immediately set upon by a group of grinning, gregarious people. They were there to sell us on their school and they did it with gusto. It was overwhelming to say the least, super saccharine to say the most. But their enthusiasm was contagious and soon I began to see the school through new eyes.

The most fascinating part of the day was meeting the other potential students and their parents. One couple we met at the start of the day seemed to be a little older than usual. I would say late 40s or early 50s and very conservative looking. They said their only child, a son, would be entering Georgia in the fall. The mother looked on the verge of tears in just saying that one sentence.

They lived in Marietta, so it was not going to be like their son was going to the moon. But still they were feeling a little apprehensive as to how their "little" boy would cope. About this time the "little" boy came up to where we were talking. To say his appearance was a shock would be an understatement. It was cataclysmic.

This sedate, older couple had a real "dude" for a son. He was six feet tall and had a head topped off with the blackest hair found on a human since Elvis discovered hair dye. He had a dangling earring on his right ear and a diamond stud piercing his left. His outfit for the day was tight jeans, tee shirt, and a black leather jacket. Still he paid his parents complete respect and attention and they basked in his love.

The next couple we met had a daughter coming to the university. They too were upset at this prospect, and with good reason. It seems the girl has a unique learning disability – that is what they called it. She can not tell directions. She gets lost driving a car in her home town. Now that is scary since the university is like a town within a town.

The only reassurance they have is that the young woman is not afraid to ask for help. They said she would just get out of her car, go up to the nearest house or store and ask directions. Maybe at the university she can leave a trail of breadcrumbs between her dorm and her classrooms.

Driving back I envied my son the thrill of going to college and meeting new people and having new experiences. I am sure it will be one of the best times of his life. And I am looking forward to meeting new people through him. People who share with us the fears and frustrations that all parents have.

'Y'all Be Careful Out There'

It seems lately every time I turn around I am hearing about more crime and more violence. Even in my protected world of Perry, Georgia the bad guys are getting active. It can really get you down and make you paranoid to the extreme. I know I have begun to hear noises in the night where I never did before.

Now I know there was crime when I was growing up in Clinton, SC but it didn't seem as close at hand. It was always something that happened in the next county or at least the next town. I don't mean that we didn't lock our house, but it was only at night. During the day the doors stayed open. Today I keep my house locked tight day and night.

But in Clinton when I was growing up we were always able to sleep with the windows open. That fresh air that came in made the best sleep on earth possible. It is something air conditioning can not replace. But today I keep my windows locked too.

My brother has refused to come into the modern age. He persists in keeping his house unlocked as well as his car. He counts it a matter of personal pride for some strange reason. I say he is aching for a break in.

He is not alone. I was at the post office in another city recently. A guy came in to buy some stamps and then went outside. He came back yelling at the top of his lungs that someone had stolen his car. He was furious. But when he was questioned he said he had left the keys in the ignition. That is like saying to the thief – take my car, please.

On top of it all the guy was mad at the post office for having thieves in their parking lot. Now that takes a lot of nerve, or a lot of stupidity.

On the same note I was at the post office in Perry the other day. A woman came in to use the stamp machine. When I went out I saw her vehicle parked in front of the building. The motor was running and her infant child was in the back seat in a car seat. Now if a thief had taken that vehicle he would have taken the child too. It only takes one time of carelessness and a tragedy like that could happen.

Even in Clinton today there is more crime. My stepmother was going to the bank a few weeks ago. As she started to get out of her car a man ran up and grabbed her purse. She held on for dear life – and that is what it could have cost her – her life! Her legs were down below the edge of the door and the man was trying to shut her into the car. It is a wonder he didn't break her legs.

Finally he got the purse loose and ran away. He hasn't been found. My stepmother suffered some bruises and a lot of anger. I asked her why she didn't just turn loose of the purse and let him have it. I mean it wasn't like she had her life savings in there. But she answered that it is just a natural instinct to hold on to what is yours.

It doesn't look like things are going to get any better soon. The world today demands that we be cautious and vigilant. It doesn't require that we get hysterical over it all. We just have to remember the phrase the man on "Hill Street Blues" said every week before he sent his troops out on the street. He said very precisely, "Y'all be careful out there." And that's what I say to you.

Beauty Is Inward And Outward

Bobbi Eakes came back to Warner Robins, Georgia a few weeks ago. She came back to visit her family but also found time to make appearance at a variety of events. These included a talk and performance for the Officers' Wives Club at Robins Air Force Base, an autograph signing at the WMAZ-TV sponsored "For Women Only," and serving as mistress of ceremonies for the "1990 Miss Warner Robins High School Pageant."

It was especially poignant to have Bobbi back on stage at Warner Robins High School, for this was where all the magic of her talent was first seen. The Warner Robins High School "Follies" Director Ronnie Barnes was in a sense the man who discovered her for he placed her and her enormous talent in the forefront of the cast of one of his shows.

The first year I saw her she was the show stopper as "Annie." In a curly red-haired wig she touched everyone's heart with her own version of "Tomorrow." It was one of those times that you are overwhelmed by talent. Not a person who saw her perform could doubt Bobbi Eakes was going places.

Over the years I had many chances to see her perform again and to talk with her about her career aspirations. She was a determined young woman, determined to make it to the top of the entertainment world. And all along the way she had the constant and total support of her family.

That is one of the brightest points of the Bobbi Eakes story, the love and support she gets from her sisters and her mother and father. Sisters Susan, Sharon, Sandra and Shelley are all beauties and grand talents in their own right. They have each had their own area of success in beauty and talent pageants.

Sandra and Shelley are the two sisters I know best, next to Bobbi. Sandra has combined marriage and a family successfully with her own career goals and that had to be a difficult task. And with each passing year she gets younger and younger looking which should make her the envy of any woman over 25. Sandra also has another major accomplishment in that she brought the family another "S," her husband, Steve. And his enthusiasm and niceness fit right in with the Eakes way of life.

Shelley to me is the funniest member of the family. There is just something about Shelley's sense of humor that cracks me up. I have judged contests with her and she always makes some comment about something that happened to her in a pageant that sets me off. And it doesn't look professional to have one of the judges wiping away tears of laughter. Shelley is beautiful and funny, and beautifully funny. Her humor is usually turned inward and that makes it even more charming.

Speaking of tears, one of my most outstanding memories of the Eakes girls happened at Sandra's wedding. Bobbi was singing a beautiful song and as she sang she cried. And that got the other girls crying, and even Sandra I think was crying. Poor Steve probably thought the world was against him but that wasn't the case. It is just that these girls are so close that their emotions rise to the surface on certain occasions.

Bobbi now lives in Los Angeles. She has a major role on the television series "The Bold and the Beautiful." And those two "B" words describe her to some extent. She is bold in her career plans and how she plans to meet her goals. She is beautiful both outwardly and inwardly. But there is another "B" word that describes her. She is "blessed." Blessed with a family that loves and cherishes her and this gives her the strength and security to pursue her dreams.

At the "Miss Warner Robins High Pageant," Bobbi sang "Home" from the Broadway show "The Wiz." It tells about how much the love of home and family means. Her family was in the audience filled with pride as their daughter and sister was on stage filled with love for them. And the rest of us were basking in the glow. Bold, beautiful, blessed – that's Bobbi Eakes.

'If This Were Played Upon A Stage Now, I Could Condemn It As An Improbable Fiction'

When I was coming along in high school the reading of Shakespeare was compulsory. I struggled through "Macbeth," "Romeo and Juliet," "Hamlet" and other of the bard's works. And I never enjoyed any of it. But now in my older years I am becoming quite a fan of the man. And that is a real surprise to me.

Now don't get me wrong. If I had the choice of seeing "The Hunt for Red October" or "The Tempest," Clancy's classic would get the nod in an instant. But I also thought the Kenneth Branagh version of "Henry V" was one of the best movies of the year.

Kids being kids, and teenagers being teenagers, I thought today's students would also run for the hills if anyone mentioned seeing a Shakespearean play. But I was wrong. I underestimate the intelligence level of today's young people and their ability to appreciate a clever witty, play.

This enlightenment concerning today's youth occurred a few weeks ago when I went with the senior class of Westfield High School to Montgomery, AL. The trip was devised by Jeanette Anderson who teaches Senior English at this school. It has become an annual event to make the trip, but this was the first time I had been included.

Montgomery is the site of the American Shakespeare Festival (ASF). This series of plays and players used to be located in Anniston, AL, until a wealthy benefactor bequeathed $21 million to build a new theater and buy grounds in Montgomery. With that kind of cash to throw around he could have said to put it in Paducah and everyone would have said "of course."

At the ASF a variety of plays are presented. There is a big theater upstairs and a smaller theater below. There is generally a Shakespearean play going in one of the theaters with something entirely different being offered in the other. This past season they have offered such diverse plays as "Cat On A Hot Tin Roof," "I'm Not Rappaport," and "Noises Off" in addition to the lineup of Shakespearean plays.

The play we went to see was "Twelfth Night." This is one of Shakespeare's brightest comedies and the production was magnificent. Still it was Shakespeare and to my mind a lot to swallow in one sitting. Not only do you have to reacquaint yourself with his style, you also have to get your mind's ear attuned to his language.

I kept looking around during the production to see if anyone was heading for the doors. They weren't. They were listening to every word and obviously appreciating it since they were laughing at all the right spots.

When the play was over some of the actors came onstage to take questions from the audience. Again I was impressed at how the young people joined in and took part. They honed in on costume meanings and other artistic aspects of the play.

Afterwards I heard them talking among themselves about how good it was. Now this is a generation which has grown up to the quick images and sounds of MTV. How could that appreciation spill over into an appreciation of Shakespeare? The answer appears to be – easily. These kids have very catholic tastes and absorb different aspects of culture in a blink of an eye.

We, the older ones, can learn from that ability to adapt and adjust. That doesn't mean I will ever like rap music, or will ever understand how Milli Vanilli gets their hair to look like it does. But I can hear "Guns and Roses" without smashing the radio, and even like everything Paula Abdul does.

Young people + Shakespeare = enjoyment. That is a formula I thought was a dream. But you live and learn. Live to see what miracles each generation brings forth. And learn never to underestimate anything the young can do.

Sore Foot Put Forward

All my life I have had good feet – exceptional feet. I can walk anywhere on them and they don't get tired. In the summertime I am always barefoot when I am at home and when my wife and I take a leisurely stroll after supper, I go without shoes.

People see us walking and are amazed that I can stroll on the pavement with bare feet. "It doesn't bother me," I say. "I have very good feet."

That is why it was such a surprise when my right foot turned on me. My big toe got red and inflamed and messy looking. But it didn't hurt. It never hurt.

I had my wife look at it. "Yuuuuck!" she said. "That looks awful."

I thanked her for her wonderful opinion and then went off to play doctor on my foot. I was sure I could heal whatever little problem I had. But it soon became obvious that I couldn't. I had to make an appointment with my doctor and get him to cure it.

At his office I was relaxed. My toe still didn't hurt but it was looking redder. A fact my doctor observed as soon as he walked in the door. "Yuuuuck!" he said. "That looks awful."

I looked around for an echo chamber. There was none.

The doctor put some medicine on my toe and told me to watch it for a week. If it did not make rapid improvement I would have to go to a podiatrist!

I had never been to a podiatrist. I had never thought about a podiatrist. I didn't know any podiatrists. But one week later I was referred to a podiatrist. My toe was still red. It still did not hurt.

When the nurse came in she looked at my toe. "Yuuuuck!" she said. "That looks awful." Obviously that sentiment was contagious. For when Dr. Bunion came in he took one look at it and said, "Yuuuuck! That looks awful." I was four for four.

The decision was quickly made that I had an ingrown toenail and that a portion of the nail would have to be removed. All I could think was "Yuuuuck. That sounds awful."

The main thing that worried me was the idea of having a shot in my toe to numb it. Can you think of a worse thing than a needle being injected into the soft tender flesh of your toe? I couldn't. So I tensed myself to wait for the great pain that was to follow.

I closed my eyes, said a prayer and waited. The pain never came. I couldn't believe it. The shots (three of them) had been given and I never felt more than the briefest sting.

"You are great," I told the doctor. "I never had shots that easily."

"Oh, I give great shots," he said arching his eyebrows like Groucho Marx, "It's the surgery you have to worry about. Nurse, get me a saw."

If there's anything I like it is a doctor with a sense of humor. He was also a liar. He did great surgery too.

It has been a couple of weeks now and my toe is back to normal. It still bears some traces of the trauma but it has survived mostly intact. I am very fortunate.

In this world were everyone has a specialty, I am glad there are podiatrists. I have always had great feet. Dr. Bunion is helping me keep them that way.

Father Doesn't Think All Women Are Bad

Now that my father is getting up in years, I have noticed some distinct changes. In his younger days he was a man of few words and no hard and fast opinions. He was always the man who could see both sides. But age has changed all that. Now he sees everything as black and white, and is constantly telling me about it.

He and my stepmother came for a visit this past weekend and once again it was time to listen to the absolutes of life. He has a favorite chair in my den and there he sits while he lays these words of wisdom on his captive audience of me, my wife, and my children.

The first absolute offered concerned smokers. My father doesn't like them. "I won't let anybody in my car with me smoke. If they don't like it they can just get out. I'm just not going to have it," he said.

"There is one man who comes over to where I am working and smokes. I have reported him once and I will report him again if he keeps it up," he continued. "I am not going to have my lungs ruined just because he wants to ruin his."

My father is long retired from his job as a bread salesman but now works for my cousin at his car dealership. He considers himself indispensable around the place and will not let anyone push him around or blow smoke in his face. That's my father – Charles Atlas.

My father wasn't through with his smoking story. "Do you know who are the worst about smoking, Jackie?" he asked.

I didn't know, so he quickly responded, "Women! Young girls and women! Just about all of them smoke. You don't see that many men and boys smoking now but you do see a lot of women."

He was really rolling now, and he continued, "Women and young girls are also the worst drivers on the road. I am on the roads a lot delivering cars and I see them all. They pass you going eighty or ninety miles an hour and just suck you up in their exhaust. It's terrible. Sometimes I just want to get on my CB and report them."

Now lest you think my father is one terrible chauvinist let me quickly tell you about his next topic – doctors.

"I never thought I would be going to a female doctor," he stated. "I thought all my life that only men should be doctors. But you know this woman doctor I am going to now is one of the best ever."

He waited to see my response, which was noncommittal. I don't know his doctor so I can't offer him an opinion.

"Dr. Patsy is full of new ideas and ways to make me feel better," he added. "And she talks to me – and better than that she listens to me. The doctor I had before her was a man and he would talk about baseball or something like that but he wouldn't talk about me and what was bothering me. Patsy is just interested in everything about my health and she answers all my questions."

He paused again to see if we were taking all this in. Then he concluded. "I think doctors should all be women. They care about you better, they listen to you better, and..." here he paused and then added with a wink, "if you need them to come to you they get there faster cause they all drive fast."

Sure, Dad, but what are we going to do about their smoking?

Laughter: The Best Medicine

Why is it that things that would not be funny outside church tend to be hilarious when they occur during the service? It has been this way all my life. From my earliest moments I can remember situations where I, or someone near me, would get overcome with laughter during the most solemn part of the service.

The first time I remember this happening was when I was around 6. My uncle was an usher and has as one of his duties passing the offering plate. He took this matter very seriously and made sure that each and every person in his section had a chance to "fill the plate."

One Sunday morning as he reached to hand the plate to the lady sitting on the end of our pew, he misjudged. The plate fell into empty space between the two of them and all of the morning's offering, most of it children's change, rolled around on the floor.

Now in writing that it does not sound so funny but on that day I remember breaking up completely. What was worse was my mother's joining me. My father and brother remained impassive while my mother and I stuffed our faces into our hands and howled. Finally my mother had to "take me out" and we made our escape. I don't think my uncle ever forgave us.

This all leads up to a story about my recent attendance at our Sunday Morning Easter Service. It was a beautiful service on a beautiful day and one I had looked forward to all year long. There is just something special about Easter and it brings out the best in everyone.

True to form my family ran late for the 9 a.m. service. When we go there our regular seats in the balcony were taken and we had to sit on folding chairs right up next to the railing.

The service progressed without incident until the minister began his sermon. Now this sermon was a very good one. I recall there was numerous scriptural references which people were following along with in their Bibles. It was a very attentive group.

I honestly was being attentive too, but I am also a bit of a wiggler and a squirmer in church. Why this is, I do not know. You can put me in a movie theater for a four hour double feature and I will be stock still. But put me in any situation where there is a live speaker and I will be in motion constantly. It drives my wife crazy.

So as the preacher preached I wiggled. And as I wiggled I dropped my bulletin. It fell on the floor between my feet. I reached over to pick it up and smacked my head solidly on the railing to the balcony. It sounded like the gong from "The Gong Show" and made me see stars.

I quickly regained my composure and straightened up. But it was a cheap crowd in that balcony hungry for a laugh. My wife started it. I could hear her chuckling like mad. I dared not look at her. Finally she got herself under control but the lady behind us had started. I could hear the giggles spreading through that balcony like wildfire.

All this time the preacher preached away without missing a beat. God love him, he never indicated any notice of the braying balcony. But the choir behind him did. You could see the whispers start as to what was going on up in the balcony.

Finally the service was over and we could leave. Women in the balcony had makeup running down their faces and men and children were red-faced with amusement. I was not amused. It had been an accident and didn't strike me as funny.

Since that day several stories have made the rounds about what happened in the balcony. The worst was that I had fallen asleep and slumped over and hit my head. Not true, not true!

The Bible says to make a joyful noise unto the Lord. Well on that Easter Sunday the balcony congregation at my church certainly did.

To Sleep; Perchance To Dream

Have you ever noticed how important sleep is to people. They talk about it all the time. At least my friends and acquaintances do. I hear comments like "I haven't had a good night's sleep in months" or "Before I die I would like to have one good night's sleep." As you can see my people are prone to exaggeration and intensity.

I myself have always lived by the old rule that the sleep you get before midnight is more important than the sleep you get after. That's why I like to sleep in the afternoon. There is never sleep so sound as that during an afternoon nap.

When I was about 12, I spent one summer sleeping the days away. Around two in the afternoon, I would open the windows in my room, turn my trusty fan on high, and sleep until supper time. My mother became so concerned that she took me to the doctor. She told him she was afraid there was something wrong, and that she didn't like my sleeping that much. What should she do, she asked the doctor. Wake him up, the doctor answered. He was a man of a few words and no nonsense.

Taking that astute advice she began to interrupt my afternoon sleep time. After a few incidents of interruption I gave up on my idea of sleeping the days away and went out and played. End of that siesta story.

Now that I am in my 40s I have real problems sleeping. I can't turn off my mind. I lay there and relive everything that has happened for the past few days and all that might happen in the future. The clock ticks on and on and I panic more and more. It is really senseless worry to be concerned about not getting enough sleep. I have always found that when you get tired enough, you sleep. But my mind can't absorb those kind of thoughts when it is screaming "Go to sleep!"

When I reach the point of absolute panic I get on the floor. Something about the hardness of the floor tends to put me out. But last night that didn't help. I had been awake for hours. It was three in the morning and I was stretched out on the floor hoping for sleep or unconsciousness to come. Then I thought I heard a noise.

Usually thoughts of burglars don't keep me awake. But last night all I could think about was that if someone broke into our bedroom they may trip over me sleeping on the floor. I have always thought I would try to pretend to be asleep if I awoke and someone was in the room. It would be hard to do that if someone was tripping and falling all over you. So I got back into bed so the burglars wouldn't stumble over my outstretched form.

I finally did go to sleep. I know I did because I remember my dream. In it my wife and I went to see Elizabeth Taylor. She had just gotten over her latest illness and was getting ready to go out on a date. I remember I was surprised that she hadn't lost weight during her latest illness but if anything she was heavier than ever. Plus she was rude. She told me she thought I had gained weight.

Those of you out there who interpret dreams should have a field day with that one. If you come up with something interesting let me know. In the meantime I am sitting here at the computer typing this and facing another night. I can hear the floor beckoning. If I dream tonight I hope Elizabeth Taylor is still fat and I am slim and trim. I can't face getting insulted in my sleep.

"Turn Around And They're Gone, Part 2"

As I write this it is three days until graduation. Three short days and my son's high school days will be over. I can't believe it! I can't stand it!

His mother and I are pitiful together. We have already started walking into his room and imagining how lonesome it is going to be when he is away at college. I'm thinking of having the room bronzed.

Even the cat is moping about. I caught her this morning going through his old yearbooks, wiping tears from her whiskers. We have a very emotional cat.

The crazy thing is that it seems like only yesterday I graduated from high school. And I don't remember a thing being sad about it. Well, some of the girls did cry when we sang "You'll Never Walk Alone," but my friends and I were thrilled to be done with it all.

I take that back. There was always my basketball playing friend, Hollis, walking about saying, "It will never be the same, Jackie."

The last time I talked to him, which was about six months ago, he closed our conversation by saying, "It has never been the same, Jackie."

But my folks weren't weeping any tears about my high school days ending. And I don't recall any of my friend's parents having the blues over the end of those years. Maybe they just didn't care as much, or maybe they were so thrilled their children were going to college that they were rejoicing instead of being sad.

No don't get me wrong; I too, am happy my son is going to college. I think he is going to have one fabulous time. But, good Lord, I am going to miss him. For 17 years I have known exactly where he was. And for 17 years I have been awake until he came home. How do you change that way of living. How do you cast him out into the wide world and let him fend for himself?

Ten minutes ago he was a little boy who read every book in sight. His mother would have to make him stop reading to go out and play. Ten minutes ago he was sitting on the sofa in the den with his feet dangling off the edge of the seat, watching the Steelers play in the Super Bowl and crying because they were losing.

Ten minutes ago he was small enough for me to pick up and hug and hold in the crook of my arm. And nothing ever smelled sweeter than the hair on his head. Ten minutes ago he depended on me for everything.

A few days ago I was driving to work and a song came on the radio. Michael Bolton wrote it but Laura Branigan was singing this version. It had lyrics that said "How am I supposed to live without you? After I've been loving you so long. How am I supposed to live without you? When everything I'm living for is gone?"

For some reason that song expressed exactly to my mind what I was feeling. You spend a lifetime living to see your kids grow up to be happy and healthy and ready to start their lives away from the home nest. But seeing them start out on their own is a killer.

How are we supposed to live without them? I know we will all manage, but it is going to be hard. And, oh, how, I just wish I could have that 10 minutes back once more.

Was It Business Or Pleasure?

Poor me. I had to spend five days at Disney World last week. It was a business trip and the locale which was chosen was the "Wonderful World of Disney" in beautiful middle Florida. It's a dirty job being forced to go there but somebody has to do it – and boy, was I glad it was me.

My wife and I stayed at the brand spanking new Dolphin Hotel. What a place! What luxury! Now I am sure Donald Trump and Ivana and/or Marla wouldn't be so impressed but I was. It was and is just beautiful. And it was so new that they were still working on portions of it even as we walked about.

The staff of the hotel is Disney sweet too. Where do they find these people and what do they feed them? They are chipper from dawn to dusk. And it never, ever gets tiring. At least not for me. I like people who speak to you when they meet you in the halls or on the elevators or in the lobby.

And they all have name tags that show they are "Bobby" or "Martie" or "Chip." It was like living with the cast of "The Mickey Mouse Club." And that is what they are called – cast members. I kept seeing rooms marked "Cast Members Only." I knew there were no shows going on around there so I was puzzled. I finally asked "Buffy" or "Skip" and they told me Walt Disney World is one big production, so all the people who work there are known as cast members.

I should have asked about the yard work. I am sure there must be people, or elves, who come out in the middle of the night and cut the grass and trim the hedges. They always look neat yet I never saw anyone working during the day. It must be Disney magic again.

Another aspect of Disney World and magic occurred several times while I was there. Parties were held at different locations and alcohol was offered in buckets. I mean you couldn't turn around without a tray of drinks being offered. But I never saw anyone get drunk or even the least bit high.

Another amazing occurrence was with the people in my business group. We were all being treated like kings, but all a lot of them could do was gripe. They griped about the wait to be served in the restaurants (even though they were getting free food). They griped about a lack of hot water in their rooms (though they were getting free lodging). Or they griped about not getting enough complimentary gifts (though we got fruit baskets in our rooms, as well as free caps and polo shirts).

Maybe we are becoming a nation of wailers and whiners. The "Me" generation has grown into a full force of spoiled adults. My folks always told me not to "look a gift horse in the mouth" whatever that means. I think it has something to do with being grateful and saying thank you.

There's a whole other world out there, full of opulence and luxury. I don't know if I could adjust to being there all the time, but for a few days in Florida it was great!

Many Welcome Couple's Baby

OK, so maybe it was a late marriage in life if you compared it to getting married when you were in your late teens or early 20s. Bess and Bernie were thirty-something. Not old by any means but not younger than springtime either. This was for both of them a second try at marriage. The first ones had not worked out but this time they were going into matrimony with both eyes open.

And it did work out – so well that they wanted to bring a child to the marriage. Even though they would be forty-something and raising it, they wanted a baby. People are having children later in life now, and the problems once inherent in these pregnancies have been overcome by modern medicine.

Still there are those who loudly asked if they were crazy. Loudly said no couple at this state in life should have a baby. It wouldn't be fair to the child – they said. It wouldn't be fair to the couple – they said. But Bess and Bernie just went on with their lives and their plans.

It wasn't easy. Well, getting pregnant was easy- carrying the baby was difficult. There was more than one miscarriage. There were more than a few tears shed. There were more than a million prayers offered. In their circle of friends and even in the community at large where they lived, the dream of Bess and Bernie for a child became one dream, one prayer, one hope.

Then a year or so ago the physical problems that seemed to have been plaguing the couple and messing up the pregnancies were corrected. Bess got pregnant again and it proceeded through all the lengths where she had miscarried before. The days went by, the weeks went by, and the months went by. Bess got bigger and bigger and the baby got stronger and stronger.

Never have I seen so many people so excited about the upcoming birth of one baby. It was the number one topic of conversation. In our Sunday School class we offered prayers for "everybody's" baby – for that is what he had come to represent.

Yes, we knew it was going to be a he. Again the modern miracles of medicine had made that fact known. It was a boy and he was healthy and everything was going to be fine. There might be a few complications along the way but somehow we all knew this one was the charm. This baby was going to make it.

Now I know there are many, many couples out there who have wanted a baby and it hasn't happened. And I don't know why it happens for some and not for others. Those are the kind of things that can drive you crazy if you dwell on them. But I think that so many prayers and so many hopes helped this "event" to happen.

Yesterday he was born and he is perfect in every way. He has a full head of hair and the most perfect skin I have ever seen on a newborn baby. He is really wonderful. And when I stood there and held him I felt like I was holding a miracle. We had all been waiting so long it seemed, but yet now that he is here it seems to have been just a blink of the eye.

So welcome to the world Baby B. You don't know yet how much you mean to your parents and to a whole collection of forty-something people who thought their days of babies would be only as grandparents or friends of grandparents. But you proved us wrong on that. You have come to give us back our youth for a few more years

– to show us again what life looks like through a child's eyes.

Wonder of wonder, miracle of miracles – it is a special day when a baby comes into your life. A day of joy, of responsibility, and most of all, hope.

Winning the Battle Of The Bulge

DIET! That word has haunted me for most of my adult life. I seem to be constantly fighting the battle of the bulges. And it has caught up with me again. Last week my doctor put me on a 1,000 calories-a-day diet.

It was my cholesterol that did me in. When I had my physical it was a little, no make that a lot, high. But then why shouldn't it have been? The day before the physical I lunched out on chicken McNuggets and french fries. Then that night I ate my share of a big pizza. My little cholesterol pores sucked it up right and left. I could hear them screaming "Thanks, sucker!" in my ear.

So here I am on a diet and everywhere I turn there is food, glorious food. Yesterday my office went out for lunch. I had to watch my close friends feeding their faces on a variety of delectable dishes. I had a salad – a good salad, but still a salad.

Then last night I was in Atlanta on business. I was interviewing a Navy S.E.A.L. The interview was running longer than we had planned so he asked me to join him for supper. Reluctantly I agreed. Reluctant because I knew I couldn't eat much.

We went to a place in Buckhead. The reason we chose that place to eat is that Dante Stephenson who owns and operates the restaurant is also a former S.E.A.L. So here we are at the club, chatting with the boss, and being inundated with delicious food.

Our table had four different types of fondue. I thought this fad went out with the 70s but it is alive and well here. There was beef, cheese, shrimp, and dumpling cut up and ready to heat and eat.

The S.E.A.L.s were having a great time eating away (I thought these guys were supposed to stay in shape!) The chub was eating soup and salad for the second time in 24 hours. But believe me it was delicious soup and salad.

Yet even in my darkest hour I knew there was a light. For when I went on my 1,000 calories-a-day diet I intended for it only to be a six-day-a-week marathon. On the seventh day – Friday – I will rest and recuperate. I will also feed my face like it is going out of style.

For lunch I will have my wonderful lumpy yummy steak at my favorite eating place. Then I will go to a movie and indulge myself with popcorn by the bucketful. One day is not going to be that much trouble and with that promise in mind I can make it through the other six.

If you are reading this and feeling sorry for the fat guy writing this, just remember that once I was thin like you. All through high school and college I just couldn't gain weight.

But one day the metabolism god said, "Sock it to him!" It was like I drank a glass of water and exploded. My buttons almost popped from my shirt it was such a rapid gain. And it has been that way ever since.

Still I have faith that the six-day Cooper diet will get me back into fighting shape. The S.E.A.L.s told me you had to have a good amount of body fat to make it in their group. This is because they are in water so much and you need that protection against the cold.

Well I am all ready for them. I have enough body fat to keep me warm through next February, but I am willing to get out of shape in order to be pleasantly thin for my wife and doctor. But if the diet doesn't work I will contact the S.E.A.L.s recruiter immediately.

'Do You Remember When...?'

I remember when I was a small child I would sit around at my parents' feet and listen to them talk – to themselves and to other people. I always loved to listen to the older people talk because they would go way back in time and tell about what they missed in the present that was so important in the past.

Now that I have gone past 20 – way past 20, I find myself reflecting on things that I miss from my younger days. Face it, there are some parts of 1990 that just don't match up with 1955. So here is a list of some of the things I wish I could see, smell, or touch once more.

I miss twilight. I know it still exists but it doesn't come into my house the way it used to come into that house on Holland Street in Clinton, SC. Around five in the afternoon the sunlight would come through my parents window and pattern their wall. The colors would be a shade of light orange and it would make the house a stiller, quieter place.

During this time my mother would be in the kitchen cooking supper and I would usually be winding down my homework. Sometimes my brother would be in the living room playing the piano which always made my mother happy.

It was a good time of day. Not the best for a small boy, but a good secure, comforting time. I miss it. My house today is shut tight all year 'round and the shades are usually drawn. No twilight gets into my house.

I also miss gullies. We had big ones in front of our house. Big drainage ditches that brimmed full with raging water when you had a real "gully washer" of a rainstorm. My brother and I would rush out with bits of paper or other objects to make imaginary boats that would flow downstream in competitive races.

For some reason I never worried about snakes or other terrors being in the water beneath my feet in the gully. I walked with a calm assuredness that it was only full of mud and other non-lethal debris. And it always was.

I miss being small enough to be rocked. I always loved to be rocked. I guess I was getting on toward huge before my mother stopped rocking me. And even today I can feel that secure feeling that was there for me when I was wrapped in her arms.

As the chair went back and forth she would sing to me those terrible songs she loved. I grew up on "Sonny Boy," a song about a little boy who died and whose parents grieved forever. Or there was another where a man killed his girlfriend and was going to be hanged for the crime. Lord knows I loved them all and would beg her to sing them over and over again – and she would.

I rocked my boys when they were small. At the least hint that they wanted to be rocked I was there. But they never let me sing them those songs. I would barely get a few bars out before they complained. Maybe mother just had the better voice or something.

Finally, I miss fresh air. We live in an air conditioned home. We never open the windows because the fresh air can now aggravate your allergies. So I don't get that cool feel of early morning or early evening air that I loved as a child.

Yes, there were a lot of things in 1955 that are gone today. But thank God for memory where we can store our treasures and then visit them again and again.

Couple Has A Second Chance

For most of my life I was a Baptist. Now I am a Methodist. But even before I made the switch in denominations I made changes in my viewpoint on some things.

One of these was divorce. Now don't take anything I write here as meaning I am knocking the Baptist faith, for some of the greatest lessons I ever learned were in the First Baptist Church of Clinton, SC. But as I got older some of my views softened.

I started out thinking divorce is a fatal sin. If a man and a woman got married and then divorced it was all over. They would burn, baby, burn, and there were no exceptions to the rule. This may have had something to do with why I waited until I was 28 to get married.

I wanted to make absolutely sure I found the right person.

But before I got married it had already dawned on me that no one can ever be absolutely sure. And even if you are sure the other person may not be. And even if you swear you will never get divorced, the person you marry might have other ideas. In the game of matrimony there are no absolutes.

What brought this all to mind was a wedding I attended recently. The bride and the groom were and are close friends of mine. When I first met her, her marriage was already on shaky ground. Although she had two wonderful children the marriage was coming to a halt.

Everything in this relationship made her feel like half a person – half a wife, half a mother, half a woman.

Then there was my friend, the future groom. He too was in a marriage that was terminal. It seemed like everything he did was wrong. He really did make a valid effort to be what his wife wanted him to be but failed at every turn. He began to feel like half a person – half a husband, half a father, half a man.

After both divorces were over the two friends of mine began to see each other as friends. They knew from the start they had a lot in common. And as they shared their experiences with matrimony they offered the other one consolation, and courage, and confidence.

Then, as in all good stories, friendship turned to love. Two people who had thought they would never, ever have that second chance again found it right in front of their noses. And soon they were engaged, and last week they were married.

The wedding was beautiful. His daughter led the procession into the church. Then came her daughter, and then the bride came in on the arm of her son. My wife explained to me that women who are getting married for the second time aren't given away again by their fathers. They are their own person and are escorted down the aisle.

The vows this couple said to each other seemed most appropriate. They talked about accepting each other as equals. And they thanked the other for giving a love that was worth risking hurt. While they spoke their vows the whole world seemed to stop and admire the love this couple had for each other.

I still am not crazy about divorce. I think there is too much of it in the world today. And I worry about the children of these marriages that fail. They are always the ones who get the short end of the stick.

But in some cases good can come out of bad. It did for my two friends. For last week in the sight of God and man they made a commitment that I know will last a lifetime. And in that church on a very special night what was half finally became whole.

Check Writers Checked Out

A friend of mine had a heart attack the other day. Thank God it was not as serious as it could have been, although they did classify it as the type known as "the widow maker." That sounded ominous to me but the prognosis for my friend's recovery is good. The main thing, his doctor told him, was that he needed to eliminate the stress from his life.

How do you eliminate stress? I mean there is stress in just getting out of bed each and every day. At least there is for me. Then there is the world news. I have to worry now about how we are going to handle Iraq and Kuwait, plus there is the economy, and crime in the streets. That is a lot to worry about – and I do. Always I do.

Then there are the personal problems with job, marriage, children, schools, grades, finances, and a million types of problems. Nobody I know is a complete expert on living so you have to sort these things out day by day, week after week by yourself.

I know there are some people who just don't worry so much. My brother tells me when he gets in bed at night, as soon as his head hits that pillow he is out. My father says the same thing. Well, what happened to my genes? When my head hits the pillow is when my mind kicks into overdrive. I go over every possibility about what I should have done and what I will need to do.

And then there are the little things. Those little obnoxious happenings that drive you crazy. My latest ulcer starter is the grocery store. I am not going to name names because it probably is true of them all, but have you tried to pay for your groceries with a check lately. No matter how often you are in the store and how often they have seen your face, when it comes to taking that check they are skeptical.

They try to explain the hesitation away by citing an infamous crime ring that is preying on the area and passing bad checks right and left. That must really be a good gang because their exploits have been heralded for months on end.

But anyway, you hand over the check and they immediately ask to see your driver's license. It doesn't do any good just to tell them your driver's license number (which in Georgia is your Social Security Number), they still have to see it. They want to know when it expires. Now why do they want to know that information? If you have an expired license does that make you a crook?

If you are like me and have a box number on your checks as your address, that is worse. Now they have to have a street address and a home phone number. Then they ask if you have a work phone and what it is. I mean, what is the logic here? If you are going to write bad checks then you certainly aren't going to give true information on all of this.

The end result is that the customer feels harassed; the company gets no good will out of the system; and the information given is probably worthless anyway. Thieves are not people who feel compelled to tell the truth. This "band of thieves" which is terrorizing the area by issuing bad checks probably has liars as it leaders.

So come on grocery stores, get a better system. You are losing customers by this policy. If you need to know all of this background data before accepting a check, then have check cashing cards issued. This used to be the way it was done and most people didn't mind making a one time offer of information.

If it doesn't get changed, people like me will continue to be stressed out by the bother of providing this minutia of information. And there is enough stress in the world without it. I can't solve the Middle East problems at the same time as I am worrying about when my driver's license will expire.

College Has Become His Second Home

He's gone to college. The day that seemed so far away for so long, arrived suddenly, and he left.

One day he was living in our house and the next day his car was gone. He was at college, and I don't think things will ever be the same again.

We have talked on the phone with him just about everyday. Oh there are a few days when we will skip a day and we are so proud of ourselves for doing that. We call him up and ask, "Did you notice we skipped a day?"

The wonderful thing is that he has been so good about all of our attention. The first week he was gone I called and offered for us to come up and have Sunday dinner with him. He said he didn't think so but thanks for asking. I could have put up an argument but I didn't.

I dropped back and compromised. I got him to promise that we would never go for more than two weeks without him coming home. If he did then we could come up and have Sunday dinner with him. He said okay. See what I mean about how nice he has been.

I have to say the phone conversations have been great. He talks about his classes and his friends and his life in general.

I never got this much out of him when I talked with him at home. But then at that time we had all the time in the world for conversations and now we only have the span of a phone call.

Its funny, but your life turns on how he sounds on the phone. If he sounds really great then I feel really great. If he sounds like he is holding something back then I worry about what it is until the next time we talk. Then if he is okay then I am okay again. Its a flip, flop and fly world but that's just the way it is.

Poor Sean (my youngest son) is really being a great sport. Of course he plans on turning his brother's room into a suite for himself. Private bath and all that you know. But Sean also has to put up with fancy food. When JJ (the oldest) was at home we ate basic food over and over because JJ is so picky. But good old Sean will humor us and eat anything.

A few days ago we had a chicken pot pie without the pie. It was an experiment. Sean took one look, one bite, and said, "I sure do miss JJ."

Fluff, the cat, misses him too. She has moped around continuously since he left. She even let us give her a bath last weekend.

That is not the Fluff I have known and loved. I have always considered her an independent cat who didn't need anyone. Well she acts like she really needs JJ. I have even considered taking her up to see him for Sunday dinner.

For the past year or so she has quit coming upstairs. She's getting older and those steps are hard to climb. But yesterday she came upstairs and looked around. It was as if she thought we had him hidden up there.

Poor pitiful Fluff, grieving like she does. Poor pitiful us, grieving like we are. This is the new normalcy of our life. It will never be the same. It will just be this way. Until Sean leaves. And then there will be a new normalcy to adjust to.

That's the way life is. One transition after another As Linda Ellerbee and Billy Joel say – And so it goes.

There's No Place Like Home...
Unless You Are A College Freshman

A few days ago I was talking with my son, the college student. We were discussing how different it is to be totally on your own at school – away from home. He was pointing out the benefits and I was making a list of the down side.

Suddenly he stopped in mid-conversation and said, "I don't mean this wrong, but I haven't been homesick at all."

He was apologizing for this fact, but I assured him it made me very pleased that he had not been. For I know homesickness is one of the worst kinds of sickness. If you have never felt it then count yourself lucky.

The first time I met up with homesickness was when I was 7 years old. My brother, who was 10 at the time, and I went to Charlotte, NC, to visit our Aunt Lillian and Uncle Eugene. It was the first time I had ever been away from home without either of my parents being with me.

My aunt and uncle had every intention of showing us a great time, but as fate would have it, the first night we were there they had unexpected company. So while the grownups talked in the living room my brother and I tried to entertain ourselves in the back of the house.

My brother was one of those kids who could be entertained watching rain fall. I saw him spend an hour one day watching the wheels turn on a little car he had bought. He did not need TV, books or movies to be entertained; just give him some string or some marbles and he could entertain himself. Me, I was just the opposite. I needed direct attention in order to be happy.

So on this night while my aunt and uncle were occupied with unexpected visitors, my wonderful brother decided to teach himself how to type. That was not my idea of fun. And as I watched him type "Now is the time for all good me to come to the aid of their country" for the one hundredth time I felt the beginning of desperation creeping over me.

My stomach literally began to ache and my throat became strained. I thought I was dying. I thought I wanted to die. I thought I wanted to go home. And I did. I wanted to go home badly – terribly! Horribly! And go home I did. The next day, after a miserable night, my uncle took us home – the typist and the most homesick little boy in the world.

You couldn't pry me away from home after that. I didn't want that awful feeling again, ever. But three years later, when I was 10, I was sent to camp for a week. Three years had not made much difference. The creeping, crawling sickly sickness was still there. It came to me on the day I arrived and stayed with me for one whole miserable week.

Throughout my life I have had some more moments of homesickness. When I went off to college I had a few twinges. When I was in the Air Force I had some more. And even today when I think back about my childhood and how life was, I get a few bursts of homesickness.

So my son need not apologize. I am happy he has so far been immune to this ailment. And I hope he always will be. For homesickness is one of the sickest sicknesses you can feel.

Hospice Is For Families And Patients

A few weeks ago I hosted a Gospel sing sponsored by the Hospice Association of Houston County.

I enjoyed being involved with the show because I like Gospel music and also because I am a big believer in the good being done by the Hospice Association.

Over and over I have heard people who have had need of Hospice services say how wonderful they are.

Hospice works with patients and families of patients who have terminal illnesses, and believe me, a family involved in that kind of life and death situation needs all the help they can get. And I don't mean just the monetary kind of help. I mean the emotional kind that money can't buy.

I was 14-years-old when I learned my mother was terminally ill. Her illness drug on for an eternal two years. In some ways it was over in a flash and in other ways it went on and on and on. Her dying was one thing. Coping with it was another.

No one can tell you how to handle an illness of this sort. I handled it in one way, my brother in another, and my father in a third. My brother became a walking saint, my father became withdrawn, and I became a wreck. I hated the way they acted and they in turn thought I was hell on wheels. But as I said, we all cope in different ways.

As a teenager the best thing for me was not discussing it at all. My two best friends never mentioned it that I can recall. With them I was free. Free of the burden of having a sick person in my life constantly. It wasn't that I didn't care. It was just that I needed an escape, and as long as I was near that house there was no escape.

That is the beauty of Hospice. It allows a way to have an escape. I wish I had had it then because my escapes from the house and from the pain of seeing my mother slowly die were filled with guilt.

Most of my free time I felt had to be spent with her. I would come home from school and go into her room and spend hour after hour listening to her relive her life for me. It seemed there were so many stories she had to tell me so that I would really know her and by knowing, really remember her. The days passed and story followed story.

It was a weird situation to live through. I had become part of an "Arabian Nights" plot whereby my mother told me the stories to ward off death. As long as there was another story to tell then the finality of death could not arrive.

And each afternoon when she finished one she would say, "Tomorrow I will tell you about when my brother broke my arm" or some other fanciful tale.

But of course one day the stories ended and the "Arabian Nights" could no longer be. Real life is not a fairy tale.

Hospice works to make the pain of death and dying easier on all of the family members. And believe me, they all need it.

Ask anyone who has gone through the experience. In a terminal illness situation every member of the family dies a little. And each person handles that death in a different way.

Flying Has Its 'Ups And Downs'

For someone who doesn't like to fly I have certainly spent more than my fair share of time in the air lately.

During the past month I made two trips to California and back, and next month I am flying to Snow Mass, Colorado, on business. The trip will involve a flight to Denver and then a quick hop over the Continental Divide into Aspen.

The first trip to California was an experience. The company flying me to California had booked me into first class. Yes, I was up there where all those "other' people sit. And I was as much in first class as you can be in first class. I was sitting on the first row right under the movie screen.

Sitting behind me was Coretta Scott King. I didn't get to talk with her because she stayed on the phone just about the entire trip to California.

I had always wanted to know who used the phone in airplanes. Now I know. Coretta Scott King does.

Anyway, as I sat down I was joined by my seat mate. He seemed like a nice guy – in his 40s and a little overweight. I figured then that he and I had a lot in common. As the plane took off he clamped his hands on his arm rests indicating that he did not like to fly and that was another bond between us.

We began to talk and I asked what he did for a living. I discovered that he was basically retired. He had worked as a stock broker but now just dabbled in things. "I guest you could really call me a 'vulture investor,'" he said.

You could almost hear the plane come to a screeching halt. My heart was pounding. Here I was trapped in the sky seated next to someone who called himself a "vulture investor." Now that was a chilling occupation.

But he soon explained that the term meant he looked for dying companies and bought their stock and revived them enough to make a profit. I think that is what he said.

With that as an ice breaker we talked all the way to California. I found that this guy, named Kenny Thomas, was like a walking twin to me. He was married and had two children (ditto); his mother had died of cancer (ditto); his father was still alive (ditto); he had one brother (ditto); the brother was divorced and was a school teacher (ditto and ditto); and he, Kenny, was the one in his family who was the sounding block for everyone else (ditto, ditto and big ditto).

We also had our names in common. I asked how he responded when someone called him "Ken." "I just don't answer," he said. "I tell them my name is Kenny and then they have to deal with that."

Anyway, while we were talking the plane hit a few bumps. This didn't make either of us feel too great. "Tell you what," said Kenny. "Why don't we just eat our way across America. That way if this plane goes down we will die happy. They will find us with smiles on our faces."

And that is what we did. We had nuts, and grapes, and dinners, and snacks, and coffee, and juices and more more more of everything. I am sure I landed in LA weighing 10 pounds more than I had weighed in Atlanta.

On the way across the country Kenny and I swapped stories. Some were serious but most were funny. We laughed so much that people came up and asked what was going on. Even the stewardess wanted in on the jokes. Coretta never asked.

Eventually our conversation turned to movies and moviemaking. It is a subject that fascinates me and since Kenny is from California it is a subject with which he is also familiar.

Kenny said he had seen the movie business pretty closely since his brother is an actor. This immediately piqued my interest since I thought I might have seen him in something.

It turned out I have, and maybe so have you. But I'll give you that information later. For now I want to relate the saga of Tom Lowell, actor – the man who had it made for a while in Hollywood.

Tom Lowell's real name is Lowell Thomas but the radio commentator already had that one registered. So Lowell Thomas became Tom Lowell. That's how those things happen in Hollywood. When he started out he was a nice looking young man, clean cut and all American. His career started in the '50s and that is what movie fans wanted at that time. So Tom had the perfect look.

One of his first roles was in a James Stewart film called "Take Her, She's Mine." He had just lucked into it by living in Hollywood and knowing someone who knew someone.

Still getting a chance to be in a movie was a real treat and fanned the flames of his intentions to be an actor.

Tom also got cast in "The Manchurian Candidate." This is where you might have seen him since this Frank Sinatra/Laurence Harvey starrer was recently re-released. In the film Tom played the young GI who had his brains blown out by Harvey in his brainwashed state. The scene of Tom with a pistol to his head was used over and over to advertise the film.

After these two minor roles young Tom was discovered by Walt Disney and was cast in "That Darn Cat" as Haley Mills' boyfriend and then in "The Gnomemobile" with Walter Brennan. Things were going good in Tom's career.

Then he landed a recurring role in the TV series "Combat." Here was steady employment in a popular show. Tom was sure he had arrived. And the notices he got from his appearances on the show were very good. So good that his agent said they should ask for a raise. Against his better judgment Tom agreed and a demand for more money was made.

The makers of the show didn't agree that Tom was so valuable. Instead of agreeing to the new salary they decided to write him out of the show. He had to film his own death scene knowing he had killed one of the high spots of his career.

After that Tom hoped to get back to work in movies based on his Disney features. But Uncle Walt was dead by now and he had run a tight ship. His actors didn't get loaned out to other studios. They stayed close to the Disney lot. So Tom didn't have a lot of contacts, and with the '60s coming in the Disney brand of movies were failing.

So began the decline of Tom Lowell's career. He had the talent still but his wholesome looks were not in demand in the shaggy '60s. He kept trying to get that "one break" again and again but it never happened. And his obsession to get rediscovered took its toll on his personal life too.

His marriage failed because he was devoting so much time to trying to revive his career that he just didn't have the time to be the husband and father he could have been.

Finally Tom semi-quit the business. He went back to school, got his teaching degree, and started teaching drama at a Catholic school in a suburb of LA, and that is where he is today.

But the dream lives on. Each summer he acts with a troop at one of the colleges in the area. And everyday he still thinks the magic might happen again. But so far nothing.

Dreams die hard in Hollywood. You hear a lot about the women there in pursuit of their dreams but you hear very little about the men. But they are there too – studying, working, dreaming.

When I talked with Kenny Thomas it was easy to see he wishes his brother's dream would come true again. I wish it would too. At least by writing this story I can show him his name in print again – Tom Lowell, actor.

Look Backward; Look Forward

"What Are You Doing New Year's Eve?"

It is hard to believe but 1990 is fading and 1991 is ready to begin. On Monday night all over the world people will look back at the year gone by and look forward in some way to the year to come. And for most of us the eve of the New Year will be a little sad because unlike the song says, it is not the good times we remember – generally it is the bad and the sad.

When I was a younger person I thought if you stayed up to midnight that you could actually feel the old year pass through you on the way out and the new year pass through you on the way in. And believing in it, I actually felt it a few times. I also thought that the first wish made in the New Year would actually come true, but life threw a few hard balls at me and taught me the invalidity of that one.

Still New Year's Eve does serve a purpose. It does force us to look back at what has gone behind, and somehow it gives us hope for what just might happen in the New Year to come. I have spent New Year's Eve grieving over a lost love and wishing she would come back. And I have spent New Year's Eve in the company of a new acquaintance wishing she would get lost. In the latter instance I made sure that was my first wish.

Then I had the best year and met the right one, and married her. Then my new years began to be full of hope.

And when our children came the wishes were always about their health and happiness. However I still saved some back for my wife and myself too.

This year, what can the wishes do for the world and for me? Lord knows I hope we get peace in the Middle East. And for all those people who have loved ones over there I pray for their safe return. And I wish the wives and children of men who are gone could know how much I admire their courage. I know there are women over there too but in my circle of friends it has been only males who have gone and left family behind.

I wish, wish, wish we could find a cure this year for the diseases of the world. As 1990 ends I have so many friends who are sick or who have sicknesses in their family. But I repeat to myself and to them that each new year brings hope. And where there is life there is hope. So hang on and hope and pray and then hope and pray some more.

And for everyone who is alone I wish that you would find the right person because no one should be alone on New Year's Eve. And being an incurable romantic I wish that every one could be with that just right special person.

So as the clock hits midnight this year let's all look back, not in anger but in love. Let's do think about all the good times 1990 brought. Let's do emphasize the positive and eliminate the negative. So when we hear Barry Manilow sing "What Are You Doing New Year's Eve?" we can answer to ourselves – we are counting our blessings and looking forward to many more.

Happy New Year!

Chapter 4

Customer Didn't Come First

Everywhere I turn the headlines are telling me the country is in a recession. Television newspeople lead off with gloom and doom each and every night. They have pounded it into my head enough that I am now convinced the economy is shot. But obviously not everyone had gotten the word. For if they had I am sure the salespeople who need my hard-earned money would be nicer to me.

Yes, the grinches who stole my Christmas spirit were the salespersons I had to deal with while making my Christmas purchases. Their attitudes were recession proof and they acted as if they were doing me a favor in waiting on me rather than me doing them a favor by shopping in their store.

Here is a true scenario of what I went through at one large department store the Saturday before Christmas. I went there to get my wife a dress. Now that is a horrendous task for any husband to undertake, but since I am a fearless soul I decided I could handle it. And I did – to a certain extent. I mean I found the right dress, without any assistance, and took it to the check out station.

Now this cash register was right in the middle of the dress department but there was no one there to run the register. One lady shopper was standing there and said she had been there for about 10 minutes but no one had shown up. I waited with her for a short while and then decided to go and look for the elusive salesperson(s).

At a register across the aisle there was a lady ringing up items. She had about 10 people to wait on. I asked where the people were who were supposed to be in the dress department. "On break," she answered. End of discussion and no further comment. She was obviously busy and had no time to chat with me.

Now I moved to a third register where there was another crowd. But this register had two cash registers so I figured it would move twice as fast. One lady was moving back and forth from side to side waiting on people who were grumbling like mad. The Christmas spirit was fighting a losing battle and fading fast away.

Only one register was being used but I could understand that since there was only one salesperson there. But then a second salesperson entered the picture. She was obviously a college student working part time over the holidays. You could tell from her smile and eagerness to help the customer. She had not become jaded like the full-time worker.

Anyway, Susie College came on the scene and dove right in. She even asked if they couldn't open the second register. "No cash in it," she was told, "Oh," she answered. She hesitated a moment and then said "Well, can't we do charge sales in it?"

"No," came the response. And when it came it was with such vehemence that any more questions were squelched. Susie College was a chastened clerk. She questioned nothing else, but went to work alternating at the one register in use while the customers stood and glowered as they waited.

I finally got to make my purchase and left the store with only bad thoughts for the company in my head. And I am sure all the others in line felt as I did. The next time we would try to shop somewhere that employed people who would treat us a little better.

One last word on this story. The dress didn't fit. When I took it back I was treated better than I was when I made the purchase. That seems to be just the opposite of what logic would dictate. Buy an item and you are treated badly; take it back and you are treated great. Someone must have left a chapter out of "Basic Salesmanship 101."

My Prayers Weren't Answered, Thank God!

Do you listen to country music? I do. It is my favorite kind of music these days.

Now that doesn't mean I can't appreciate all the other forms of music – but country is my favorite.

It wasn't always that way. I used to think country was strictly for hicks but then I started listening to the words and I was hooked.

Many times I have thought that I could write a country song. I am forever hearing one or another and thinking I could have written that because I have lived that story. But somebody else always beats me to it. And my career as a country music lyric writer remains on idle.

Still if I were going to write a song it might be about my life as a young man.

When I was in my 20s I started going with a young woman named Patty. Patty was fine. I was fine. We were both fine. The only thing not fine was a place called Vietnam.

When I got of school I knew I was going to have to join some branch of the service or I was going to be drafted. So I joined the Air Force. And that meant I had to leave my home in South Carolina.

In my mind as soon as I joined up I knew I was going to have to go to Vietnam. And I didn't want to leave without having someone to leave behind. By this time I had met Patty. We hadn't been that serious but with Vietnam looming I wanted to marry Patty so that she would be waiting when Jackie came marching home.

Lord knows my prayer was for Patty to say yes to me and for me to go off and serve God and country as a happily married man.

That was what I prayed and prayed and prayed. And sure enough Patty said Yes. And sure enough we planned our marriage. But somehow we just never could find the time to get married. One thing after another kept getting in the way.

I was really angry. I had sincerely prayed to get married and now it was not happening. I became a single, bitter man who was angry at God and everybody because my prayers had not come true.

Well, Patty and I never did marry. The wonderful romance just could not survive the differneces we had. Eventually Patty married someone else. She was the second one to do that to me. I was zero for two.

After I got out of the service I stayed in the area and one day when I was downtown I spied Patty in the grocery store.

Once what had been fine, was fine no more. Life had weighed heavily on her or at least that was the way she looked. Or maybe I had just seen her through the eyes of love before.

Well my eyes were wide open now and I thanked the Lord he had not answered my prayers.

And that brings me back to the start of this column. Garth Brooks has a number one hit song on the country music charts. It is called "Unanswered Prayers." I could have written it but Garth or some friend of his beat me to it.

It tells the story of another man who prayed for a true love to last and last, but it didn't. Then he married someone else and he was very, very glad that God didn't answer his prayers.

So, the song says, some of God's greatest gifts are unanswered prayers.

For some reason we are not always the best judges of what is best for us. I'll vouch for that. Amen, hallelujah, pass the biscuits please.

Flying Is Really For The Birds

Anybody who knows me knows I do not like to fly. I do not trust planes. I don't understand how they stay in the sky so I am a basket case each and every time I have to board one. But planes are the name of the game as far as travel is concerned these days.

Since I have been going from coast to coast so often lately I have built up a goodly number of miles on my frequent flyer card. Pretty soon I will be able to make a round trip somewhere for free. It is a little ironic that the prize I win by flying so much is a chance to fly some more.

Anyway, right after the war started in the Mideast, I had to go to Los Angeles on business. I didn't want to go. If I could have gotten out of it I would have. I was afraid of flying. I was afraid of terrorists. I was afraid of sabotage. I was afraid pure and simple.

Still it did dawn on me that we should not be held hostage in our own country. If we all sit in our homes afraid to go anywhere then whoever these terrorists may be, they will have won. So I made my reservations and I planned my trip to LA.

When I arrived in Atlanta to board my flight the security was tight. The lady checking baggage actually apologized for the inconvenience. I assured her they could check any of my bags no matter how much time it took. I just wanted the flight to be as safe as possible. Not everyone shared my feelings. There were a couple behind me griping about every security precaution taken.

I made my trip to Los Angeles with no problems. The flight was smooth and the trip uneventful. We even left and arrived right on schedule.

Coming back I was not so lucky. After I had boarded the airline and gotten into my seat I was joined by the person sitting in the seat next to mine. He had the window seat. I had the aisle. I never sit by the window if I can help it because I don't like to look out.

A few minutes later a man entered the plane, came to where I was and said I was sitting in his seat. He showed me his ticket, and sure enough, he had the same seat number as mine. We called the stewardess and she took both tickets to try to find the reason for the mix-up. Soon she was back saying the computer had goofed and would one of us mind sitting in another vacant seat which she had located.

I refused to move. It wasn't that I was trying to be mean but I never change seats on a plane. I figure fate assigns me a seat and if I change around I will be tempting fate to zap me. So this guy was not going to get me to budge. He tried though, Lord knows he tried. But I had squatter's rights. I was in that seat and it was going to take him and three others to get me out of it.

He didn't have three others with him so he finally gave up. He wasn't happy. Maybe he had the same feeling about the fate assigning seats that I had. Still if he had known what I went through with the guy sitting next to me he would never have wanted the seat.

I was feeling really obsessive about terrorism and I saw a potential candidate in every stranger. Especially on this plane flight. One of the elements that created my fear was the person who sat next to me on my flight home from California. He looked normal enough, but looks are deceiving. Shortly after he took his seat the fear quotient began to rise.

While we were waiting for everyone to board "Mr. X" became fidgety. Finally he crawled over me and went to the front and talked with the stewardess. They had an animated conversation and then he came back to his seat.

A few seconds later he spied another stewardess and he went back to the front of the plane and talked with her. Then he came back and took his seat again. Shortly thereafter another stewardess motioned for him to come back up to the front of the plane. He went back up and talked with her and then came back to his seat.

I was getting suspicious by now. And my suspicions got even higher when the last stewardess and a man with a walkie talkie motioned for him to come talk with them. They had a fairly long conversation and then he came back to his seat.

By this time I had to know what was happening so I asked. "I guess I should have just kept my mouth shut," he said. "I guess I am probably paranoid with all you read in the newspapers."

I asked him what he meant and he responded, "I thought I saw a guy come through the side door on to the hallway leading on to the plane. You know that ramp you come down to reach the side of the plane."

I knew the one he was talking about, but I didn't remember seeing a door off it where someone could come in. Still if he said they could, well I believed him.

"Now they want me to walk through the plane and see if I can pick him out," my seat partner continued. "Like I should know what he looks like. I wouldn't know him if he was sitting right across from me."

While he was telling me this the guy with the walkie talkie was walking up and down the aisles of the plane. He finally came back to the front, went out the side door, and the plane started up.

"I guess he's satisfied," my neighbor said.

Satisfied! I thought. How could he be satisfied? And how could this idiot sitting next to me have thought he saw someone sneaking on the plane and not have gotten a good look at his face. If he was suspicious enough acting to create a fear in the man why couldn't he have watched what he looked like and where he went.

While I was thinking these thoughts the guy next to me turned towards the window and promptly went to sleep. Leaving me awake and panicky all the way to Atlanta waiting for the bomb to go off. Which it didn't. Which is what the airlines thought all along. The guy next to me – the sleeper of the year – probably never saw anybody sneak on the plane anyway. He probably thought it was a great joke. But it wasn't for me. And it wasn't for the airline personnel, I'm sure.

But everyday there is some idiot who does something like that. This time my path just happened to cross with his. I hope it doesn't happen again.

You Can Bet I've Got Other Worries

Several years ago when I was living in California, a lady came up to me at a soccer game in which my son was playing and asked me a question.

She asked, "Didn't I see you at the Methodist Church this past Sunday?"

"Yes," I answered.

"Well, aren't you the man who writes those movie reviews for the newspaper?"

"Yes," again I answered.

"Well, are you a Christian or not?"

"Yes, I am."

"No, you aren't. You can't be and go to see those trashy movies," she said. Having made her decision then and there anything I had to say to her was not going to change her mind.

Well, I am still going to the movies and I am still a Christian. Somehow God and I have worked it out. But a few weeks ago I heard that you can't be a Christian and be for the lottery. Now there's a definite statement for you and one with which I just don't happen to agree.

I am not going to argue that the lottery is the greatest thing that could ever happen to Georgia but I also do not view it as the first step towards Sodom and Gomorrah. Yet the churches and all are talking about the lottery as the next plague against mankind. I have never seen so many letters to the editor against something; so many preachers preaching against it; so many politicians crying out about its harmful impact.

Where are these people when there is a case of racial bigotry and hatred resulting in death, harm, or just hurt feelings. If we want to talk about life and death, let's talk about the abortion issue. If you think abortion is wrong then you are actually working
against murder of unborn children. But I don't hear these zealots raging against this wrong.

To take it further, what about the homeless, the unemployed, those ill with AIDS or other terrible diseases. Let's get upset about those situations and rant and rave. If there is going to be a bandwagon let's load it down with a subject of more importance than the lottery.

If Jesus Christ were physically here on earth today I think he would be working to feed the poor and house the homeless rather than campaigning against the lottery. He certainly had his priorities in line when he lived here. He didn't rally against Caesar and all his ills. He just rolled up his sleeves and worked at curing the sick and feeding the hungry.

Priorities is my point. I would not argue with anyone who thought the lottery was wrong. But I would argue that with all the ills in the world today the lottery is way down on the list of things that should be crusaded against.

Let's keep the fervor going but let's focus on something that really needs to be fixed – like hunger, homelessness, and illnesses of the world.

These are just my views – the views of an imperfect Christian – one who goes to movies and who has bought lottery tickets. I don't toss stones. I can't afford to. Can you?

Sixteen Years Of Memories Are Sweet!

Sixteen years! It can't be 16 years. It was only a few moments ago that he was born. A few precious, wonderful moments that have been fun filled and happiness heavy. But I guess the calendar doesn't lie and it has been 16 years since Sean was born on St. Patrick's Day in 1975.

JJ is his older brother, and after he was born I didn't think there could ever be a little boy I could love as much as him. He was bright, loveable and wonderful. And with his brown hair, brown eyes, and dark skin he was his mother made over. And I loved him even more because when I looked at him I saw her.

But then came Sean. Unlike his older brother who came when he was overdue, Sean came early. It was like he just couldn't wait to be born, didn't want to miss out on any fun that might be happening. He let his mother know at supper one night that he was on his way and look out.

I remember thinking it couldn't be working out this way. JJ had been induced. We had plenty of time to get ready. I wasn't ready at all for this new baby to be born. Sean wasn't listening.

I rushed back into JJ's room and got him up. Norine Jones, the wonderful woman who had been babysitting with him all his life, had told us to bring him to her whenever we had to go to the hospital. But my very precise JJ was having problems about going there.

"I can't go see Rine in my pajamas," he cried. "I have to have on clothes."

I tried to assure him it was all right. Terry and I have always felt you should discuss things with your children. But after several attempts to persuade him I just grabbed him up and headed to the car where his mother was waiting. She had called Norine and she was waiting for JJ's arrival – even in his pajamas.

After we deposited JJ with Norine we headed to Macon. I was approaching warp speed with Terry yelling for me to slow down. Then when I would slow down she would tell me to speed up. It was a scene out of a movie – a horror movie.

At the hospital I called my stepmother. She had said she would come when the baby arrived. My father had planned his vacation around the due date so he could bring her to Perry. But the birth was happening before the due date and he couldn't change his vacation. So, my stepmother, Florence, who never drove anywhere by herself got in the car and headed from Clinton, SC, to Perry.

At the hospital things were progressing and soon Sean was born. I swear I think he came into the world laughing. And where JJ's hair was dark, his was blond; where JJ's skin was olive, his was fair; and where JJ's eyes were brown, his were blue. And when I looked into them I loved him even more than I thought possible because in him I saw the me I used to be.

Children are wonderful. They give you back your youth. They give you your immortality. They give you your hope. This past Sunday we celebrated Sean's 16th birthday. Family and friends gathered to wish him well. And as he stood to receive their good wishes I observed that his hair is still blond and his eyes are still blue. And just like the boy I once was, he is still laughing.

I'd Be Happy Driving Miss Daisy

A few weeks ago I got a new car. My 16 year-old son took over my old car, which I loved, and I ended up with a new one. It takes me a while to adjust to a new vehicle and this one is no exception. I am trying to figure out the little niceties it possesses and discover the ones it lacks.

The worst thing I have found so far is that the clock does not show the time when the radio is on. That really frosts me. I am a constant clock watcher when I am driving somewhere. My old car would show the radio station and then flip back to the radio station number.

I also have not figured out how to set the clock. Daylight Savings Time came about last week and I am still in the past as far as my car clock is concerned. On my old car you set the time by using the "scan" and "seek" buttons. This one does not operate that way. I don't know how it operates but the "scan" and "seek" are not the answer.

Let me explain I bought this car sight unseen from my cousin, the car dealer. I always buy my cars from him that way. I tell him I need a new car. He tells me what he has and we go from there.

When he told me about this car he did mention that it did not have power door locks. I didn't think that was a big thing, but now having gotten the car, it is. Believe me it is! It was so, so easy pushing one button and having all the doors in the car locked or unlocked. Now it is push, push, push and push.

Still what really is important to me is how the car drives and this one does drive like a dream. I don't care what a car looks like as long as it glides along smoothly. For you see I love to drive. I know some people would rather dig ditches than drive but I absolutely love it.

When my family and I moved to California we drove out and back. I had such a good time I would have gladly driven to Hawaii. If you mention that you want to go to Atlanta, I will drive you. I have been known to drive up there and back just to see a movie. What's a couple of hundred miles when you love to drive?

Most of the time when I drive I am alone. So I sing. I sound great in a car. Marie Osmond and I have sung "Meet Me In Montana" so many times we are on the charts. I know all of Reba's songs by heart, and right now I am learning "Promist Me You'll Remember" from "The Godfather, Part III." Harry Connick Jr. is teaching it to me.

My friends at the library have urged me to listen to audio books in my car. I haven't committed to that yet. But I have discovered "talk radio." It is great. You hear all kinds of things on the air from sports to entertainment.

The worst thing about driving though is it makes me long for the days when I smoked. Yes, even I used to have that nasty, filthy habit. I would drive, drive, drive and smoke, smoke, smoke. The miles flew by through my nicotined singed fingertips. Those were the good old days when I was immortal and so were my lungs.

When I retire I think I'll become a driver like "Hoke" in "Driving Miss Daisy." Across the country I could go in a well-tuned car, singing with Reba and having the time of my life.

After Graduation, There Are The Memories

Tears and Joy, Joy and Tears that will be with us forever through the years. And we will smile and say that we will remember Graduation Day. Those or some words like that were part of the song we sang on my graduation day.

I haven't thought of that song in years but now that Graduation Day is here once more it has been playing in the jukebox of my mind over and over. And over and over I have gone back to the days surrounding my high school graduation.

It just dawned on me that I never think of my college graduation as being my *Graduation Day.* That is purely and simply high school – a high school thing. Maybe because it is so traumatic. I mean you are being pulled from the womb of friends and family to go to the cold, cold world of being an adult.

At least that is how I felt. It wasn't that I wanted to stay in Clinton, SC, forever, but I did worry how life away from there would be. Plus my girlfriend was still in high school and I would be separated from her. And the biggest fear of all I had was that things would never ever really be the same again.

It hasn't been. There is never another time of your life which is quite as intense and as innocent as high school. Your friendships are the closest, your emotions the most close to the surface, your highs the highest and your lows the lowest.

The entire summer after we graduated my friends and I spent the days working and the nights reminiscing. It was like we were trying to crowd a lifetime of memories into three months. We were thicker than glue and able to do things together without the petty spats that had troubled us on and off before.

At least most of us were. There were a few exceptions and one of those was Sandra Davis. For included in the days following my graduation was the night Sandra Davis fell out of my car. It is amazing how that one incident has stayed in my mind all these years. It happened as we were driving around after church one Sunday night. We always drove around after church – but back then gas was cheap, so why not drive.

There were three of our friends in the back seat. My girlfriend Elaine was sitting beside me in the front and Sandra was sitting next to her on the outside next to the right car door. We didn't have seatbelts in those days so I was always reminding people to lock the car door. While I was driving I looked over and noticed Sandra had not locked hers.

I told her to mash down the handle, which was the way the door was locked, when for some strange reason she lifted the handle up. It was just as I was going around a curve and the momentum of the turn pushed her out as the door opened.

Elaine grabbed her hand and Sandra clung for dear life. There was a car behind me so I couldn't slam on the brakes. So while I brought the car to a stop, Sandra bounced around on Elaine's hand like a corkscrew. It wasn't funny then and in reality it isn't funny now, but I can always remember in my mind Sandra bouncing up and down as we rode along.

It ruined her Sunday shoes, I can tell you that. And it tore a hole in her dress. But she didn't suffer any broken bones or cuts that required stitches. She was very lucky. But she was mad! I mean she was really mad. Like it was my fault she didn't know how to lock a door.

I remember her yelling at me that she was glad I had graduated and that she was glad I was leaving Clinton and hoped I would never be back. Well, I did come back, but I don't remember ever seeing Sandra after that.

Memories are amazing. You don't ever know what is going to pop up in your mind. Like Sandra Davis and her monumental flying feats as she bounced along outside my car. Sandra Davis and my graduation – a time of joy for me, a time of tears for her, but a time we both have remembered all these years.

Father's Day Brings Back Fond Thoughts

It is strange how becoming a father sneaks up on you. I don't mean the actual act of being a father, but rather the reality of it. My sons are now 16 and 19 and it still surprises me at times to realize I am actually a "father."

I guess it is because I have been a son all my life and only a father for the past 19 years. And there is still a man in Clinton, SC, who is the "father" in my mind. "Father's Day" makes me think of him and not of me. Since last Sunday was "Father's Day" I did a bit of reflection on what he has meant to me and what I, hopefully, have meant to my sons.

My first recollection of my father was how big he was. I can remember standing on his feet and being walked around our house. I could put both my feet on one of his and still have plenty of room. And I can remember him lifting me over his head with me yelling and screaming – for him to do it again! I never worried about falling, I always felt secure.

My father, or Daddy as my brother and I call him, was not home a lot when I was growing up. He worked six days a week from early morning to late afternoon. But when he was home, he was home. He didn't golf or hunt or do much of anything else. He was either at work, at church or at home.

My father doesn't have much of a temper, never has. I could probably list on one hand the times I have seen him mad. As a child I think I only saw his temper one time. That happened on a Sunday afternoon.

Some kids in the neighborhood and I had gone up to the school yard that was near our house. It had a playground with swings, a slide, hang bars and a merry-go-round.

While we were playing there some older kids came to play. Or rather they came to torment us younger kids. They demanded we leave the playground because they wanted it to themselves.

Now I was never Mister Brave when I was a kid, but I did like to swing. And at this age it was one of my very favorite things to do. So, surprisingly for me, I said NO! Well, this older kid (he was probably a sixth or seventh grader whereas I was a first or second grader) proceeded to toss me out of the swing.

The toss didn't really hurt me but the swing seat came back and caught me in the back of the head. I saw stars and yelled like I was dying.

I hollered even louder when I reached back and touched my head and found blood! Off we all ran for home with me crying all the way.

I have always had a touch of the melodramatic about me so I am pretty sure when I got home I climbed up on our side porch, held out my bloodstained fingers, and choked out a sob. Whatever I did was enough to make my daddy see red. As soon as he heard our story he jumped up from that porch, grabbed me up, and headed for the school yard.

Now my mother was not at home for some reason, so she couldn't calm him down. And me, heck I didn't even try. I wanted him to go to the school yard and clean house. But when we got there the older kids saw him coming and ran, scattered like the wind. And it was a good thing because my daddy was mad.

I heard a song by Ray Stevens on the radio the other day. It was called "My Dad Could Beat Up Your Dad But

He Wouldn't." That is always the way I have felt about my father. I never actually saw him act out of anger but I always knew it was there in reserve if I needed it.

Sunday School Boasts Many Friendships

I love Sunday School. I really do. Well, maybe I just love my Sunday School class. For nearly 20 years now it has been a high point of my week to be there surrounded by a group of people I really like. Preachers have come and preachers have gone but my good old Sunday School class has remained the same.

Oh, we have had new people come in and even some old people leave, but somehow the consistency and atmosphere of the group has basically remained the same. And so has our routine. We come to class around 10, mix and mingle around the refreshment table, sing a song or two, and then have our lesson.

Sometimes the refreshments are just coffee, and sometimes the singing is pretty weak – but the coffee is strong. And always there is a variety of lessons being taught by three men and a little lady.

That is the composition of our current group of teachers – three men and one lone female. I am one of the men who teach and we rotate one Sunday apiece. That basically means one Sunday School lesson a month which is not a heavy burden for any of us to bear.

One of our teachers is a lawyer but you wouldn't know it from his lessons. None of that stern lawyer stuff for our class. We hear from him about the beauty of nature and the goodness of life. He delves into his own life and brings us fitting analogies about raising kids and being a good parent. I have never heard one of his lessons when I didn't learn something and I have quoted him more times than he can imagine.

The second male teacher is a former athlete. He still looks like one. That and a pilot, which he is also. When he teaches he brings us guidelines to live by. They are methods and means by which we can be successful in the business world or successful as Christians. Plus he always has a funny story to add – I mean really funny stories. And they too always have a meaning that is appropriate.

The little lady is one of the newer teachers. She brings a feminine viewpoint to our class. I don't think it was especially easy for her to join the male society of teachers but she is a real trooper and a valued member of our team.

The three men are real hams and can ad lib for an hour or more on any subject. Our female teacher had to learn to do that. The first lesson she taught was right by the book and lasted all of 10 minutes. We are supposed to go for around 20.

That didn't happen to her again. The next time she taught she went right up to the bell. And she did it by brining in some side stories about what was going on with her family and her coworkers. It was wonderful.

We got to know her a little better through these stories and she got to relax as she brought this personal aspect of her life to us. She still stayed near the subject matter of the lesson but she now expanded it a little to encompass what had gone on in her world.

I am sure that somewhere out there, there are learned professors and Bible purists teaching Sunday School. I am sure they are serving God in a wonderful way. But in the Christadelphian Class of the First Methodist Church of Perry we are having good Christian fellowship.

We are also eating fattening food, drinking good hot coffee, and learning about human and spiritual values from everyday people who once a month share their experience.

I love Sunday School, at least my Sunday School. Come join us.

To Hear...Perchance To Dream

Legend has it the legendary Andy Warhol once said in the future everyone will have at least 15 minutes of being a celebrity. For many people the future is now. Television shows like "Sixty Minutes," "Rescue 911,"and "Unexplained Mysteries" feature stories on everyday people and give them their fleeting time of fame.

For others talent is the key. Such is the case with my nephews Bo and Todd Cooper. These two young men are in their 20s and have been pursuing music careers in Nashville. Both are songwriters as well as singers, plus Bo plays keyboard and Todd plays saxophone.

In the past Bo has been a part of the Imperials while Todd has performed with Kim Boyce. Both of these are Christian groups and that is where Bo and Todd have focused their music. For a while that was a limited audience but lately such artists as Amy Grant and Michael W. Smith have crossed over to appeal to the mainstream.

Last week Smith appeared on "The Tonight Show with Jay Leno." Yes, all America could see and hear him sing his songs. And backing him up – on national television – were my nephews Bo and Todd. They had a share of their 15 minutes of fame and looked and sounded like true professionals. I think this is the start of a big career for them.

Even I had my taste of celebrity this year. It wasn't on a national television show, but rather on local radio. For five months I hosted a call-in/talk show about movies, videos, television, etc. My voice went out over the airwaves and people responded. I loved it.

Being on radio is very unique. The only way people relate to you is through your voice. They don't know what you look like; they don't know how old you are. As far as they knew I was in my 20s and had a head full of hair. It was like being younger all over again.

Of course people inevitably would say to me when they found out I was the person who was on the radio, "Gosh you don't look a thing like I imagined!" Therefore I began to keep it my little secret that I was the host of the show. I preferred for people to dream me up in their imaginations. It was more fun that way.

Think about it. If you listen to radio at all, do you know what the people you listen to look like? Haven't you created a full image of what their physical appearance is? I know I have.

So if you listened to "Jackie K and the Marvelous Movies" the five months it was on the air and you thought the host was a tall, muscular, drop-dead handsome guy – you were right. For those months of the show he was alive and well and living in Macon. Now he has packed his bags and gone back to the surf of Malibu.

Of such are legends born – Hi yo Silver awaaaay!

All In All The Trip Was Good
But Not A Drop Did I Drink

A few weeks ago I went to Acapulco. I hadn't planned the trip in advance, it just happened. It was a business thing and I got invited and before I knew it there I was. Acapulco was not one of those places on my wish list to visit. But in truth no place outside the confines of North America is on my list and I am not real sure about Canada.

I am not a world traveler. I don't like to travel. I don't like to fly and I don't like to go anywhere where English is not the primary language. English is not the primary language in Acapulco – and you have to fly to get there.

Many years ago I won a cruise on the Mediterranean on a game show. My wife and I flew to Greece and then sailed around the Greek isles for 10 days. We were the envy of all our friends. I didn't want to go.

It ended up a fairly good vacation except that I got badly sunburned and the ship's doctor did not speak English. I didn't hold that against him. He spoke Greek. I was in Greece. If I wanted a doctor who spoke English I should have stayed at home.

I didn't need a doctor in Acapulco, but a lot of people who were with me did. But they didn't have the benefit of Mercy. Mercy is a lady I know who was on this trip. Everywhere I went I would look over my shoulder and there she was. And every time she spoke it was with the voice of gloom and doom.

The first thing she told me was that by no means was I to drink the water. "Don't even let the water from the shower get in your mouth," she warned. "And use only bottled water to brush your teeth."

I did as she said. I sang not a note in the shower in Acapulco for I was so afraid I would open my mouth and some water would rush in. I was even afraid to swim in my pool. Yes MY POOL. The hotel were we stayed had a pool for every room. Now there's a first. But I was afraid to swim for fear some of that deadly water would get in my mouth and I would be sick.

As for food, Mercy told me not to eat any salad because that had been washed in the water and the germs would be on it. She also advised against any kind of meat, especially pork. My options for eating were quickly shrinking. Wisely I had packed almost a case of M&M's in my bag. That is what sustained me while I was on my visit.

My room was air conditioned – thank God! I don't know how anyone could survive the heat and humidity without air conditioning. It was intense. I kept my room at the frigid mark. But each time I would leave it for any reason someone would come in, in my absence, and turn it off. It was as though they had binoculars trained on my room.

Now having said all this negative about Acapulco, let me add it is a very beautiful place. Plus the people there are very friendly. Those of you who like to travel would probably rate it as tops.

As for me, I think I will stick to traveling in the good old USA. There are exotic locales here that have escaped me. As a matter of fact I hear Minot, ND, is beautiful in the summer. I can hardly wait!

Disney World Marks Two Decades

For the past 20 years whenever anyone mentioned vacation in this area you immediately thought of Disney World. It's close; it's always changing; and it is the one place everyone loves. And for some reason it has always appealed to me more than Disneyland. I lived in California for two years and never ventured into Disneyland, but I can't count how many times I have been to Disney World.

The first time I went there was in March 1972. It had opened in October of the previous year and everyone was talking about it. So I, my pregnant wife, and her 13 year-old brother made the trip to Orlando. And when we entered the gates we were overwhelmed.

We stayed for hours and still did not see it all. But we did meet Mickey Mouse and we did get to see "The Jackson Five" who were also visiting the park that day. Who would have thought that years later Michael would be the one to have his own spectacular exhibit – "Captain EO!"

This year my wife and I went back to Disney World for the 20th anniversary celebration. If anyone knows how to put on a party, it is Disney. And if any celebration can draw a crowd, it is one at Disney World. The place was packed with the President and Mrs.Bush, other celebrities, members of the media, and everyday people.

What amazes me the most is the constant enthusiasm of the people who work there. They must have mountains of medical bills for hurting cheeks because they smile, smile, smile. And where do they find all of these people with names like Chip, Chad, Amy and Sunny? I didn't see a single soul named Shirley or Arthur.

Usually these people are welcoming you with a "hello" or a "how are y'all?" But to show the international flavor of Disney World you got greeted in 99 different languages. At least I think they were greeting us. They could have been saying "get lost" or "beat it" for all I know.

Disney World used to be the size of a city when all they had to offer was "The Magic Kingdom." Then they added "Epcot" and later the "MGM" section. Now it is the size of a county. And a big county at that! We went to all three sections plus a visit to all the outlying work areas.

It is hard to think that my children have never known a world that didn't have Disney World. As far as they can remember there has been that enchanted place in Florida where people stay happy and things remain shiny new. Of course it is an illusion but in our world today it is nice to have a dream. I sure am glad old Walt had his and did something about it.

I'm Unsettled By Changes

I don't like for things to change. I don't like for people to change. I don't like for situations to change. I don't like change period! And in this world it is so true that the only thing constant is change.

I can remember all the way back to when I was 3 or 4 and was at home with my mother – alone. My father would come in from work and my brother would come in from school, but for most of the day it was just me and her. And I liked it that way. Therefore when it came time for me to go to kindergarten I pitched a fit. I didn't want my life to change. And it did.

I also remember sitting with my high school friends on a night before we were all to go our separate ways to college. We had formed a thick, thick group of boys and girls who were comfortable with each other. We put up with bad jokes and good put downs. We were as close as close could be. And when one of us said "It will never be the same again," I knew it was true.

This hatred of change has been one of the reasons it has been so hard for me to see my boys grow up. I like being a family unit of me, my wife, and my two sons. The outside world can rant and rave; grow weak or strong; do whatever, but inside my castle moat I am content. Still college and the like require me to break up my family unit. It will never ever be the same. And I don't like it.

I like the innocence of children. I like to watch youngsters being as open and as sweet as only they can be. They have no guile and no ulterior motives – for the most part. They are just children acting as sweet and as unspoiled as they can. But then I see the world reach out for them with the lure of drugs, or alcohol, or adult relationships for which they are not ready. And I grieve for them and for all of us who lose something when this kind of temptation is succumbed to by our children. I don't want them to change but some do. And I don't like it.

Now as I get older I am more confronted with death among friends, relatives, and acquaintances. I don't like death at all either, but at least it is absolute. Once a person is dead and gone that is it. There are memories but there are not any meetings again to remind you of how much you miss the individual. With changed relationships you still have the hope that things might be the same again. But they rarely are.

Where I work there is a tight unit of employees. I like them and I hope they like me. We have been together as a group for some time now, but last week we had one of our members transfer out. It almost killed me. I had thought this group would be with me for the long run. At least until I retired. Then they could do whatever they wanted. But that was a foolish dream. Circumstances usually dictate change and they do it with fair regularity. People come and people go.

The lady who worked in my office has gone now. She will meet a new group of people and hopefully they will take her in and make her as happy as we did. And I am sure we will get a new person in my office who will be as nice and compatible as the lady who left. But it will never be the same. And I don't have to like it!

There's Much To Be Thankful For

Here we are entering the Thanksgiving/Christmas holidays spree, which is generally the time of my greatest depression of the year. So before I become a morose recluse let me put down on paper a few of the things for which I am most thankful this year.

I am truly grateful to be living in a land of religious freedom. We take that so much for granted year after year, but it is one of our greatest rights. Still I wish I didn't feel at times that my rights of religion are being subordinated to the rights of non-religion of others. From my point of view my forefathers came to this country to give me a right to pray at ball games or at high school commencements, etc. I don't think they envisioned those rights being abridged by the words they put to paper.

I am always thankful for my family but at Thanksgiving I am reminded to be even more thankful for them. They are the people who love me because of who I am and, more importantly, in spite of who I am. My wife and two sons will endure with dignity my moods over the holidays and my non-thrills connected with the holiday air.

Sometimes during the holiday season I have a tendency to become touchy-feely to the extreme. I am by nature a person who shows his affection through hugs and pats. But at times I am worse than others. Although it is great to have a hug from me now and then, a constant percussion concert on your back during church is not always welcomed. My youngest son, who sits by me, bears up under this type of heartfelt affection with grace.

I am thankful for my friends. I don't always show this but I truly am. As I get older I tend to want to stay within my family unit and not venture out as much as I did early on. So making new friends is not something I do easily, but I cherish the old ones I have.

My wife says I demand too much of friendship and I do. I want it to be forever and mostly on my terms. I want it to be always there whether I ask for it or not. And I want people to act like I want them to act, which is not really fair. But in return I am the most loyal of friends. I will do anything for my friends. An I am a constant friend. So it is not like I give zero in return for everything.

Lastly, I am thankful I have a job. In my case several jobs. But I need to feel secure and being a workaholic of types gives me that peace. I don't know what I would do if I was one of the many, many in our area today who don't have a job. It would drive me nuts.

At this Thanksgiving time I am aware of several people who do not have steady employment. Through no fault of their own are they unemployed. It is just the circumstances of the economy. And it could just as easily be you or me who is in this predicament.

The people I know who are in these circumstances are living out their lives with dignity and faith that something will turn up. And I am sure it will. I pray it will. But in the meantime I just want to go on record as saying I am thankful for being able to earn an income that pays my bills.

All of us complain at times about where we work and what we have to do. We have become too secure in our surroundings.

Yes, Thanksgiving is here and we all have a lot to be happy about. Maybe some more than others, but in truth we all can count some blessings. So take the time this week to think over the good things in your life.

And then take the time to say thank you to your family, friends, and most importantly, your creator.

Today's Technology Is Almost Frightening

The world is becoming more and more of a complex place for me. I have never been and probably never will be a person who understands machines. My knowledge of anything with moveable parts is limited from the start and usually does not get any better.

Now I am at least a person who can pump my own gas. And I can check my oil. But that is it. I don't tinker with cars, and pray every time I put the key in the switch that it will turn on and I can go ride. When I have a problem with a car I end up telling the mechanic that it made a ping, ping, ping noise or went chichachick. I invent my own language as I go along.

A few years ago I got a computer and it completely puzzles me. How or why it operates is one of the big mysteries of life. Luckily it just does. You turn a switch, the screen lights up, and you type. That's the glory of, computers.

This year I got two more gizmos. I got a telephone answering machine that does everything but cook. I mean you let the thing do its thing and it will tell you how many calls you got when they came in, and generally what they wanted. And it is all done by this guy with a neutral voice who lives in there.

One of the greatest things about this machine is that if you forget to do anything with it you are supposed to, it tells you. For example: when you have heard all of your messages it tells you that you have just heard the last one. Then if you don't rewind, it tells you to. And just as a reminder it asks if you want them erased.

The only thing that scares me is that someday I will come home and there will be a light saying I got seven messages. I will push the switch to hear them and "Mr. Telephone Man" will say, "You got seven messages but they weren't important so I erased them." It could happen, you know. That man who lives in the machine might just get bored and want to try something different.

My other mechanical gift was a car phone. This one came as a complete shock to me. I thought my wife was going to give me a new answering machine (see paragraphs above) but she decided to really surprise me with a car phone. I bought the answering machine for myself.

The funny thing about getting a car phone is the reaction it brings about in others. Some were nice about it. Well, the nicest reactions were the ones I got from others who already had car phones. The ones who didn't have one said things like, "A car phone! I can't believe it!"

My brother, who has the tact of a tree, said, "A car phone! I wouldn't have one. I hope I never get to feeling so important that I get a car phone." Well, hell will freeze over before he gets a call. Or maybe I should give him one as a gift and see if he feels so unimportant that he won't take it.

I have to admit I felt awfully yuppie using it. But what the heck, it is fun. And my wife got it for me so I could call her on my way home from trips to Atlanta and not have to stop at some roadside phone.

The problem is that it is so easy just to pick it up and call. The first day I had it at work I had to call and say, "I am at the red light getting ready to get on the interstate. What's for supper?" That ease of calling will probably last until I get the first bill. Then call shock will set in, but fast.

Well I had better close this for now. My answer machine man is telling me that someone is calling me on my car phone. It will take me hours to figure out how to answer that one.

Age Is Just A State Of Mind

One day I was 16. The next I was 24. A couple of more days went by and I turned 50. That is how fast time seems to move for me. Honestly, last week I was in my 20s. I think I am involved in some kind of time warp – or I am dreaming all this and I will wake up and it will be 1970 again.

But in this dream state, or whatever, I have turned 50. It happened on Friday the 13th. Talk about a double whammy! But then you consider the alternative to not turning 50 and that is death, so you pick yourself up, dust yourself off and move on.

Still, on your 50th birthday strange things happen. You get cards and calls from people you haven't heard from in years. I got a card from a woman who grew up with me in South Carolina. She sent me a picture of the two of us all dressed up and going to a dance. This was when we were about 14 years old.

On the card she wrote, "You were my first boyfriend. I was so fat and you were so handsome." In truth she was a little heavy at the time as the picture showed. I think I am going to write her back and say, "Are you still fat? I am still handsome." Let her have her dreams.

Another friend of mine sent me an article from a newspaper. It featured a story on my friend Hollis, who is a school teacher. The article was about his teaching career and showed three pictures of him.

One was from our high school yearbook when we were 17. He was thin, bright-eyes and had a head full of black hair. The next was from 1973 and showed him to be balding and wearing glasses. The last picture was a recent one and showed a slightly overweight man with no hair on top but a white beard on his wrinkled face. He looked like Father Time.

Now that is depressing. I look in the mirror and see a face still youthful. But maybe mirrors lie. Come to think of it, I did have some pictures made lately. I didn't buy any of them because they made me look too old. I thought it was just a poorly taken picture. Sure, and that is what happened to Hollis too.

There was a lot I was going to accomplish before I turned 50. I was going to write the great American novel. I was going to win an Oscar for a screenplay. Those two events are still in the future. But at least there is still a future.

On my life journey I have accomplished other things I wanted. I wanted to find the right person and get married – and I did. And I wanted children – and I got them. All the other dreams pale in comparison to those wishes.

So now I am off on the adventure of my second half century. With the rapid technological advancements which are being made there's no telling how long I will be around. And if the second half is anywhere close to being as good as the first, then bring it on.

I am going to live, live, live 'till I die. And with faith, family and friends the journey of life that is left to me is bound to be a good one.

Epilogue

Well those were good memories from some good years. But as I look back now from the perspective of 2001 it is with a tinge of sadness. My father who dominated a lot of these stories is gone. He died in the year 2000. But as one life ends another begins and there is a granddaughter in my life. My son Sean and my daughter in law Paula have given me a wonderful gift. Her name is Genna Ray Cooper and when I look into her blue eyes I see the soul of her great-grandmother who was named Margaret Virginia Cooper and who was called Gena by those who were closest to her.

Life continues to be a wonderful journey. I hope yours is too. As for me, I face each day with the hope that more adventures await me down the road. As always the chances and choices of the journey of life continue as we ease on down the road.

Jackie K Cooper